From **Lad** to **Dad**

How to survive as a pregnant father

From **Lad** to **Dad**

How to survive as a pregnant father

Stephen **Giles**

Editors: **Richard Craze**, **Roni Jay**

WHITE LADDER PRESS

new tricks for old dogs

Published by White Ladder Press Ltd
Great Ambrook, Near Ipplepen, Devon TQ12 5UL
01803 813343
www.whiteladderpress.com

First published in Great Britain in 2005

10 9 8 7 6 5 4 3 2

ISBN 0 9543914 7 0

British Library Cataloguing in Publication Data
A CIP record for this book can be obtained from the British Library.

Designed and typeset by Julie Martin Ltd
Cover design by Julie Martin Ltd
Cover photograph by Judy Hedger
Cover models: Ceri and Peter Baker
Printed and bound by TJ International Ltd, Padstow, Cornwall

White Ladder Press
Great Ambrook, Near Ipplepen, Devon TQ12 5UL
01803 813343
www.whiteladderpress.com

To my Dad

Acknowledgements

This book wouldn't have been possible without the help and support of a number of people – above all Lindsay and 'the boy'. I'd also like to thank David Burke and Steve Fountain for their time and criticism, and the surveyed fathers for their help in providing new and surprising angles. Finally, thanks to Roni and Rich at White Ladder for making the idea work.

Contents

Information Panels

Introduction

Nine out of 10 fathers are present at the birth of their child. The other one out of 10 might be really squeamish, very busy, extremely forgetful, or stuck in traffic. Or they might just be clinging to the traditional attitude that the father's job climaxes when he does, that his role is over as soon as he rolls over. This book isn't for them. It's for everyone else, the many thousands of men every year who want to get stuck into a life-changing experience.

The role of a pregnant father is as big as you want it to be. It's not just about being there at the birth – there's a whole new world of scans, tests, hospital visits, antenatal classes, multiple challenges and infinite shopping trips. There are families to handle, crises to solve, names to choose, fears to calm and lives to change.

However much, or little, involvement you want to have, the pregnant father's role is totally unscripted. We make it up as we go along, succeeding now and then, screwing up here and there, and sometimes we blunder like idiots onto the sensitive toes of our partners. But we do appear to get there. Somehow.

This book will provide the support you need to handle the entire role without crushing toes along the way – from the doubts and fears you might have before your baby is even conceived, through the strange and sometimes freakish world of pregnancy and medical care to the unknown horrors of the delivery suite and that unbelievable moment when you finally get your hands on the new life you helped to create.

This is not just another guide to supporting your partner; it sets out to help specifically with your emotional and practical needs. Sure, some of those are going to help her too, but she's got a lot of people on her team – you're the one who could be left with the feeling that you're completely and utterly alone.

In fact, that might be just what you're going through right now, depending on how far you are along the road. Alone, thrilled, scared, jealous, overwhelmed, intimidated, excited, anxious – we've all been there and if we haven't been there yet, we'll get there soon.

All too often these crucial emotions get ignored as the father-to-be is sidelined and stereotyped by medical staff or by relatives and friends who stick to another old-fashioned belief – that pregnancy is all about the woman. Is that fair? Well, it's true that she's got the physical burden, but frankly you've still got to live with her, to cope with the physical and emotional changes that she's going through. Most of all, you've got to transform yourself into a father, to learn how to be responsible for another life that depends on you for its existence – and that's not going to happen overnight.

So this is both a personal and practical story of pregnancy from a man's viewpoint. The personal part comes in the shape of the journal which I kept immediately before and during my wife's pregnancy with our first child. It draws on my experiences and those of people I spoke to at the time. It is immediate and honest, which is a cop out way of excusing all the wrong headed comments, outbursts and moments of sheer desperation that I reckon I must have shared with most men in my position.

The practical aspect of the book is in two parts. First, it's in the advice that helped me through this momentous time. While putting together material for this book I discovered a tonne of shared experience and frustration among fathers-to-be. I have addressed as much as I can, not with cast-iron answers but with suggestions of things that worked for me, and for others.

The second practical part of this book comes in the form of snippets of information that I found useful, or that I would have loved to have known at the time. These also draw heavily on the feedback gained from a survey of new and expectant fathers which was carried out for this book – and which gave me access to a wide cross section of knowledge and advice. My thanks go out to everyone who helped make this a truly broad sweep of experience.

Of course, everyone's experience of pregnancy is unique. But because of the way fathers-to-be tend to get viewed in our society, you may be coming to this book feeling a bit isolated, maybe even a bit lost and detached from the whole pregnancy. I guarantee you won't leave it with that feeling. Here is the proof that you are not alone. Nor are you useless, powerless or redundant. You're the daddy, almost. And absolutely nothing beats that.

Chapter One
Let's Get It On

I blame Christmas. This apparently harmless holiday is actually a cover for dark forces who want to keep the planet populated. Happy, childless couples the world over gather with their families to have the same sentences banged into them – 'Christmas is for the kids' and 'children help to make sense of it all'.

Yeah, yeah, I get the picture. The older generation are tired of trying to make the day magical for their cynical, 20-something offspring. There's not much joy in trying to photograph the look of innocent delight on the face of your goatee wearing, marketing manager son as he unwraps his novelty latte set. I see why the ancients yearn for a grandchild to take up the wide-eyed role in this spectacle.

But do they have to be so crushingly obvious about it? Nothing puts you off sex so much as your parents expecting it of you. This year, for some reason, they have forgotten their duty to remind us to get shagging. Which, naturally, has made us think seriously about starting a family.

Lindsay and I have been together for about eight years, married for six, and pretty happy with it. The idea of a family has always been at the fringe of our relationship. We've followed the well trodden route of buying cats and then treating them like children – albeit children who shit in a box. We even bought dogs and treated them like children – albeit children who shag pillows. But, until now, coping with the disgusting habits of our pets has been enough of a distraction to keep the idea of actual children at bay.

Now we'll be put off no longer. Of course, it's just words at this stage, which means it's pretty easy to be blasé about the whole deal.

•   •   •

Or is it? Just a few days have passed since we agreed to start trying and already I can feel the pressure creeping into sex. I've been drawing up mental pro and con lists. I'm not really worried about the child, because that's such an abstract concept I can't take it in. I'm more concerned about the fact that, whatever happens as a result of our 'trying', my life is set to change.

Scenario one is that Lindsay doesn't conceive for a long time. I've heard it can take around two years to hit the jackpot anyhow. What if it takes us longer? I'm not old, not really old, but I will be in, say, five years. I've already started to read those magazine ads for book clubs and I linger by the slippers in shoe shops.

Worse than that is the fear of what failing to conceive could do for our sex life. I'm pleased to say that I've always found sex to be fun, spontaneous and, well, sexy. The introduction of thermometers and astral charts would surely be very, very bad news. I don't want to have to start worrying about what pants to wear or the temperature of my bath water. Then there's the dreaded checks of bodily functions. If I'm discovered to have a low sperm count will I regret wasting so much of it as a teenager?

We have friends who've been trying for children for a while and the wait does seem to have a profound effect on them, both emotionally and physically. Though I admire their resolve, their sex lives appear to have all the glamour and excitement of a tax return. Sometimes the long wait for a baby can change things, particularly relationships, when desire slips to determination, to resentment and even recrimination. Even people who cope with the emotional burden can't escape the cost in time and money.

It seems cynical to consider years of potentially miserable waiting right at the start of what is meant to be a wonderful experience. But, as with travelling on British trains, the destination must be put out of mind; what counts is surviving the journey. If we aren't mentally prepared to face frustration and possible failure then we aren't ready to try.

Till birth us do part?
Testing your relationship

The impact of trying for a baby isn't only felt in the bedroom, of course. Whether you hit the spot first time or spend years trying, the overall result is, hopefully, the same – a baby. And that's when the commitment is really tested. You often hear about couples 'staying together for the children', or 'having a baby to save a relationship' but I seriously doubt whether either is a conscious decision. What they both show is that a baby is a tie, something linking you and your partner together emotionally and financially for the life of the child. That realisation made me stop and think about the strength of my relationship.

It might seem odd to be considering such things at the same time as making this lasting commitment, but it is a key part of the process. Can you honestly picture yourself with her in 20 years? If you can't, and you're not comfortable talking that through with friends or family, have a confidential chat with a relationship counselling service like Relate – you'll find them online and in the phone book – the peace of mind really is worth the effort. The more secure you are that this is the right way forward, the more relaxed you will be later in the pregnancy, when the stress increases and your relationship might be seriously tested.

Scenario two is much more frightening. What if Lindsay becomes pregnant before we're ready? OK, before I'm ready. And how and when will I know that I am ready?

The biggest question in this scenario is what would change if she became pregnant? Would I suddenly be unable to jet off to South Africa for the bridge jumping championships? Would my career as a professional waterskier fail before I've had the chance to pull on my first wetsuit? Would I age prematurely and would my politics swing wildly to the right? Probably.

In all honesty, my life isn't so dramatic that a baby would interrupt the relentless flow of adrenaline. The closest I ever get to dangerous sport is running with scissors. In fact, I'm a bit of a lazy bastard and no amount of trying to pass off middle age spread as puppy fat will make me seem more youthful. I suppose I'm as ready as I'll ever be for fatherhood. But that doesn't mean I want to admit it to myself just yet.

Excess baggage
Freedom and the new arrival

It is definitely worth sitting down and making a list of all the things you've done in the last five years – all the holidays you've taken, all the last minute getaways you've fitted in. Then put a tick against each one you wouldn't be able to manage with a baby. Repeat the exercise for future plans and ambitions.

I guarantee that, in terms of travel at least, you're a lot more flexible with a nipper in tow than you thought. A friend of mine has just returned from a cross Africa trek with his young family, and others have chalked up trips to

Morocco, Jordan, South America and the wildest recesses of Canada. Sure, it takes a bit more organising, and the luggage grows, but you don't need to start booking through specialist, expensive agents, or committing yourself to Disney every year – just deal direct with the hotels and resorts you plan to visit. It's the best way to be sure you're getting what you want. It is usually one hell of a lot cheaper, too.

A couple of weeks into the new year and already life is different. I've never considered myself to be a particularly attractive man. I'm not ugly, but I don't have the blemish free purity of the movie star or the rugged roguishness of the rugby player. I look more like a movie star who's just played a particularly violent rugby match. Yet my wife has never found me more sexually attractive. If trying for a baby is going to continue at this frantic pace and frequency, perhaps it would be good to let it run for a couple of years.

Lindsay's hormones might be leaping around at the moment, but I can't honestly say that I've experienced much change. Except for the whole sex slave thing, of course. We even plumped for the sure-fire passion igniting weekend away to celebrate our anniversary, though any procreative effort was probably scuppered by the fact that I drank an unfeasible amount.

Drinking heavily is a near unconscious way of saying that I'm not coping too well with the demands of prospective parenthood. To be more precise I'm shitting myself at the idea. And the drink doesn't help there, either. Any way up it's a bad move, as excessive alcohol is reckoned to have a negative effect on fertility. Is this my subconscious at work?

I do think about the baby a lot now. Whenever we go to a restaurant, or the cinema, or just out for a coffee, I try to picture a little bundle of red faced screams and tears with its attendant nappy bags and cumbersome 4WD push chair, and I wonder whether we'd ever be able to do the things that we enjoy again. I can cope with losing the big things in life – like that two seater sports cars I always dreamed about – but I don't know that I can cope without the simple pleasures.

Reality bit even harder on the way home from our anniversary weekend when Lindsay declared that she 'felt pregnant'. She didn't offer this as a matter of fact, we haven't been trying long enough to know whether she's even missed a period yet. It's just instinctive, another example of her shift to some higher mental plane, while I'm still just relishing the extra sex. She was keen to test her theory.

In a bizarrely self-conscious act, we stopped at a supermarket some miles from home to buy a pregnancy test kit. This brought memories flooding back of buying my first packet of condoms. It still feels naughty to admit that, though we've been together some years, we are actually having sex. At least I didn't park in the 'parent and child' spaces.

Testing, testing, 1, 2, 3
How to handle pregnancy tests

Tricky business, the pregnancy test. They come in various forms, most popularly the little white stick which looks like an electric toothbrush which your partner pisses over. It's better if she doesn't do this in the dark, in a room with other electric toothbrushes. Trickier still is the question of whether this is something that involves you at all. The surveyed men were divided on the issue – though the words of one correspondent sum it all up neatly, 'trust your partner's instincts'.

If she wants to involve you with the test, that's great, but you both need to be prepared to cope with the despair of a negative result. If she wants to do the thing in her own time, it might be that she thinks it would be easier to cope with a negative result without announcing it to you. That may or may not be true, so you'll have to be vigilant just in case she needs a bit of support after a negative test.

Whatever she wants to do, don't take offence and don't push it. There's no right or wrong way to approach tests, just the way that suits her. You're going to need to be ready with the bubbly or with tissues, to be able to celebrate, commiserate or just keep silent. Told you it was tricky.

As soon as we got home Lindsay disappeared into the bathroom and I paced the floor like a 1950s caricature, longing for a pipe stem to chew. As I paced, I glanced around me and conjured images of our tiny home being invaded by a squawking, demanding child.

Our little house is pretty basic, barely big enough for the pair of us. I could hear the neighbours crashing pots and pans in their kitchen the other side of the thin wall. I pictured that wall resounding to their frustrated thumps as the baby launched into another 3am tirade.

This is too bleak, I decided, as the toilet flushed and broke my ghost train of thought. Try to focus on the wonderful reality of fatherhood, the joy of unleashing a unique, potential filled life into the world. Think positive.

"Well?" I said, trying not to show my own emotional balancing act.

"Negative," she sighed.

"Never mind," I said, holding her. Inside I was relieved, not because I hadn't wanted her to be happy, but because I hadn't expected my response to the test to be so uncertain. I can't believe that I have come so near to creating a new life and yet I am still questioning the whole idea of whether we should be trying for a baby in the first place.

A life sentence?
Making sense of the future

Creating a new life is the closest anyone will come to playing God, so it's small wonder some of us get a bit stressed about the idea. It opens up a whole set of philosophical questions – should I bring a child into the world, is it just selfishness, or even accessorising? Am I just trying to keep pace with Kevin from Accounts? Does the planet really need another mouth to feed? Of course it does. OK, so Mr and Mrs Hitler should have just watched a video instead, but for every rotten egg there's a Gandhi or even a Jonny Wilkinson.

It's like pulling a cracker – you don't know what you're going to get, but without the bang you'll never find out. Of course, not every father-to-be gets the chance to ponder the great issues, a fair number of pregnancies are surprises, to both mum and dad. It can be hard to accept that you've created this incredible thing without any conscious decision. In fact, nothing can make you feel more detached from the process.

But it is still vital to go through these thoughts and fears, even if the baby is already on its way. Shutting them out because the result is inevitable won't work, and there aren't many concerns that can't be dealt with between you and your partner. Playing God means taking responsibility, but at this stage that only means being true to yourself, so look at what worries you and make sure you deal with it.

The negative test has given Lindsay a more thoughtful air too. In the weeks since she took the test, we haven't talked about it as much as we should, mainly because I'm petrified of creating an 'issue'. The more we discuss it, the more it will become a matter of stress and that's going to be bad. But she's an impatient person and she's also used to being in control. The idea that her body can play tricks on her has come as a bit of a shock.

It may be this shock to the system that's making her ill. She's been totally run down for a while and we're off on holiday in a few days to the Highlands of Scotland. I'm hoping that the heady combination of winter sun, sea, sand, sex and scotch will revitalise her. At least it'll give us the chance to talk about things, and it might give me the opportunity to get my head around the idea of fatherhood.

Just a couple of months in and I can already see how crucial it is to limit stress while trying for a baby. Anything that threatens the future becomes a real problem, which is bad news as Lindsay works in the declining manufacturing sector and my income as a freelance writer is sporadic at best. So we're not exactly big on stability. If we let work worries crowd our lives then it'll be even harder to allow time for baby making, but if we don't worry enough about work we won't provide a secure platform for the future.

So how much stress is acceptable and how much will hamper our attempts at conception? Again, medical opinion suggests that excessive stress means less chance of doing the business. It seems like such a delicate balancing act – no wonder they call it the miracle of birth.

•   •   •

Until today our Scottish holiday has been relaxing and quiet. Our evenings have been marked by huge meals which I have attacked with all the gusto of a fat bastard while Lindsay has pushed the deep-fried haggis around her plate as if it was, well, deep-fried haggis.

She's maintained that she's alright, and she hasn't seemed too bad, except for the lack of appetite, but I know her well enough to sense that she's been troubled. This morning, as we drove the hundred miles or so to our final hotel of the tour, we eventually talked about it.

Rather than having a lot of worries that were making her ill, Lindsay's sole concern was the illness itself. Running through the symptoms, she started fretting about the reasons for her loss of appetite, her tiredness and lack of vitality.

We'd got as far as that stunning bit of landscape that's been spoiled forever by some arsehole of a council official erecting 'Monarch of the Glen country' signs everywhere when Lindsay, who had been lost in her thoughts for a few minutes, turned to me.

"I could have something really horrible," she said.

"No," I diagnosed, expertly.

"There is another possibility," she added. "I could be pregnant."

My instinct was to remind her of the failed test, but, in a rare moment of tact, I held back. However small the hope of pregnancy might have been, it was possible, and any hope was better than her alternative.

So we stopped at a chemists, bought another kit – without blushing this time – and headed for the hotel. We blundered in with our baggage, material and emotional, and Lindsay headed straight for the bathroom. I began my familiar pacing and tried to work out what I was going to say to console her.

A couple of minutes later she came out of the bathroom with a perplexed smile. She didn't say a word, just stood back and let me through the door. The tiny testing kit, like a junior chemistry set, was spread over the tiled surface. Lindsay held up the test and the instructions. I looked at the pictures and back at the little strip. Positive. Pregnant. And about to change everything, forever.

In the circumstances, there was only one thing I could say. Bending closer to the tiny beaker of amber liquid, I nodded. "I've not seen your pee before."

• • •

I am a god. I'm Hercules. I'm a Beckham free kick. I am Superman. I'm a caveman. I am the Walrus. Without wishing to underestimate Lindsay's involvement, I did it. Me. I decided to father a child and I've damn well done it. First time, no questions asked. Fantastic, fan-bloody-tastic. I have found my vocation as a breeder of generations. Out of my way, you puny mortals, for I am The Procreator.

I feel a little drunk.

• • •

I feel better now. God it's been a strange day, from desolation to ecstasy to reflection and now to apprehension.

For much of the day I've been wallowing in the sheer delight of knowing that I can do it. It's a feeling divorced from any of the realities of impending parenthood, but I don't give a shit. I've just enjoyed being singularly, unashamedly masculine. It's a feeling of sheer power, of wanting to hunt and gather, or at the very least ring room service.

It's an odd feeling, and as the intoxication has worn off, I've started to feel a queasy, uneasy disorientation. In the days of terraced football grounds, you could be swept up by a wave of fans charging forwards to celebrate a goal, or sideways to start a battle. There was nothing you could do about it, and if you were propelled into a metal hurdle or a concrete pillar then that was your problem for standing too close. All afternoon, I've enjoyed the feeling of surfing helplessly on the tide of events, but now I'm on the lookout for the concrete of reality.

"Darling, I'm... petrified"
Reacting to the news

This might sound weird, but a common feeling I've heard that fathers-to-be experience just after getting the good news is despair. Nothing prepares you for it, even if you have had years to gear up. Part of this strange emotion might come from the fact that it appears to be the end of your practical input, and the beginning of a new and frightening part of a journey which you no longer control. You're expected to be excited and delighted, yet at the back of your mind are all the things that could go wrong, making you feel guilty for your joy.

For me, it was literally a life changing moment, more than my 'I do' or even my signature on the mortgage agreement. And that is a hell of a lot to take in at once. Don't misjudge a few negative feelings at this stage, as long as they are balanced by the positives they are a big part of preparing yourself for the rockier parts of what's to come.

My mood has hardened and set like stone this evening. Until now we've ordered a bottle of wine with dinner each evening of the holiday and Lindsay has sipped a half glass without much conviction while I've drained the rest. Now we know the cause of her ills I can't help but sense an expectation that the wine should disappear from the table altogether, a symbol of our joint commitment to a healthy pregnancy.

I'm determined to show my support, but also to show that I'm going to remain the same. Life is changing around me, roles, responsibilities and plans are floating like dust in a shaft of light and I need something to keep me steady, a pivot for this new world order. Cheap wine is a pretty crappy pivot, but it works for me – or at least it did tonight. In the end, I ordered it, Lindsay declined it, I drank it, along with a couple of whiskies and a beer or two for good measure. Now I feel dreadful, sick and excited at the same time.

Cigarettes and alcohol
Changing your habits

This is another odd one – with the men I've spoken to split into hardened factions. On one side are fathers-to-be who launch into pregnancy with a puritanical spirit, out go the fags and booze and for some they never reappear, not even after the birth. A greater number limit the cigarettes but not the alcohol, and some take the attitude which I've expressed here that it is an important issue of independence. My attitude changed pretty quickly, but that was down to a totally different circumstance.

The only way to deal with the issue is to hit the facts – if you smoke near your partner, it may have an effect on the health of your unborn child, whereas your drinking may not be good for you, but it doesn't have a direct effect. So if you want a drink, drink. If you want to smoke, accept the possible consequences or go outside. Things are more complicated for your partner. She can't step away from the child for a fag break, she may cause real harm by carrying on, but it might cause dangerous stress if she has to stop. If she is giving up and you aren't, you're probably going to be doubling the stress on her.

The National Childbirth Trust says that giving up smoking is the best gift a mother can give her unborn child, and that may be a good way of looking at it from the father's perspective too. If you decide to kick the weed, but you want a bit of moral support, check out Richard Craze's *The Voice of Tobacco* (White Ladder) for a totally realistic and non-patronising account of kicking the habit. Drinking isn't so black and white, because the odd glass might be fine for her – it's healthier to have one or two drinks and no stress than no drink and a whole load of stress.

But again, you need to be sensitive – if you're nailing pint after pint and she's sipping her fifth lemonade of the evening, you're going to get the bollocking you richly deserve. I think I got it wrong, making something that's already tough for my partner into an issue of independence. Moderation might have been a better option, and it would have got me into a lot less trouble. Isn't hindsight wonderful?

I woke this morning sharing my bed with the mother of my child and the mother of all headaches. To say I've been hit by the reality of this enormous, incredible event does no justice to reality's powers of brutality. Reality has dragged me from the comfort of my home, around to the back alley, where it has proceeded to kick the living shit out of me. As if that wasn't enough, it then forced me to drive to the grey, cold city of Perth to look at baby clothes.

Two things have become immediately apparent. Firstly, no matter how rich and successful we become, we will never be able to afford to dress the poor little sod in anything grander than a flour sack. Secondly, we are the only prospective parents or indeed actual parents to shop for clothes.

Mothers-in-law and aged aunts hunt in packs for bootees and bibs, even reluctant grandpas skulk listlessly around romper suits, but no one of our age is anywhere to be seen. Where are these people and why aren't they buying clothes for their children? Why, more importantly, are they entrusting the clothing of their child to freakish old people capable of cooing over miniature tank tops?

Our questions were answered, in part at least, at lunch. I was promised fried chicken as compensation for the shopping, and so we crammed into Perth's busiest fast food restaurant and slid into the luxury plastic seating next to a large family party.

It was chaos. The adults were surly, sulky and irritable and their hideous children bickered and squabbled like sewer rats over the remnants of the meal. Two toddlers squirmed and bucked in their buggies like convicts in the chair. One of this pair let out a low, menacing, desolate whine, a perpetual, unwavering soundtrack of misery to accompany our food. For the first time ever, I left my chicken unfinished.

As we sat in the car I shuddered and shook my head slowly at what might have been a vision of the future or a vision of hell. Lindsay looked across at me and smiled.

"They don't all end up like that," she said, her tone somewhere between reassuring and seeking reassurance.

"God, I hope not," I said. "I really hope not."

It really spooked me. I've spent this first day after the positive test wandering in a kind of daze, looking in horror and awe at fathers with their children and wondering what the hell I'm going to make of the whole business. I know there's nothing strange about this – it's just part of the process of moving from the theory of having a baby to the reality of becoming a father. But am I going to be as witless as some of the specimens I've seen today? Will I be able to restrain myself from imposing my views on the poor kid? Will I make them support my team and follow my uncertain footsteps or will I force the little soul to become a lawyer or a doctor, or something else 'worthwhile'? Will I be a pushy dad or a laid-back dad? Will I be just like my own dad or the complete opposite?

Back at the hotel my fears for the future were channelled into a surge of practicality. I decided that we needed to contact the doctor at home to get an appointment as soon as possible on our return. I am fairly sure that we need some medical tests before anything can be officially recognised, so we got the number and I badgered Lindsay into making the call.

This is the first time I have taken command and Lindsay, normally a strong willed individual, just let me. It is a small thing, partly liberating, but mainly petrifying – especially as my belief that the doctor is the next step is based on things I've heard on TV and on the gut instinct that as doctors, like butchers, are known by their surnames, they must therefore be important.

If we are going to be led by this kind of half-arsed attitude for the whole nine months, we are in some serious trouble.

The whole nine months (and then some)
What not to say

I think this is the only time in my journal that I refer to the pregnancy as 'nine months'. I stopped doing so mainly because I didn't want to get my balls kicked into my stomach. Pregnancy, as any book, expert or bulging woman will tell you, normally takes between 38 and 42 weeks. Most go to full term at 40 weeks. That isn't nine months, it's nine and a bit. Don't ask me why those couple of extra weeks are such a matter of stress, they just are. So take this piece of advice to heart – never refer to the pregnancy as nine months, especially not as 'only', or 'just' nine months. You'll thank me. And so will your balls.

Now that the holiday's over, we've got to face up to the fact that our parents must be told. Lindsay thinks we should keep the baby a secret until it is around 16 years old. It's the only way to give the poor little blighter a chance of getting away without having to wear knitted bonnets. That won't be easy, so the alternative is to tell the family early, which gives them a chance to calm down before the birth.

It ought to be a process full of joy and delight, but we're really not looking forward to it. The first step is to stop off on the journey home and tell Lindsay's sister, who's been trying for a baby for a while, and who may have genuine reasons to be a bit distressed by the news that we seem to have started a family almost without effort.

It is hard to curb our excitement sufficiently to appreciate that other people may have personal reasons for not celebrating with us. We could adopt the selfish attitude that nothing counts beyond us and the baby, but that would just show an ignorance of fact.

"I've got some news"
Telling the world

Telling people your good news involves another emotional balancing act. The surveyed men were split once more – with half deciding to tell family as soon as possible and half waiting until 12 weeks to tell everyone. All but one of the men surveyed avoided telling everyone immediately, which shows a lot of restraint, but also quite a lot of the worry that exists in these crucial first few weeks. You'll need to pull off the same trick you managed with the testing – you've got to be led by your partner's instincts, but you've also got to keep hold of the situation.

If the worst happens and she loses the baby, everyone you've told will have to be given the bad news too. So you need to juggle the joyous high with the stone cold prospect that this could be one of the one in five pregnancies that don't make it. The majority of these end before 12 weeks, so holding back a little now may save much more pain later.

On a different and slightly more palatable note, it's also worth remembering that a 40 week pregnancy is actually one hell of a long time. For most of that time you'll be on the sharp end of a tonne of unwanted advice and criticism from everyone ranging from close family to complete strangers. Waiting until 12 weeks to break the news allows you to exist in your little bubble of happiness for a little bit longer. It might give you the time to get your head around what you plan to do before bossy Auntie Pat weighs in with what you should be doing.

Our visit began awkwardly enough. I stood in the living room, chatting edgily about football with my brother-in-law while Lindsay went to help with the preparations for lunch. Eventually her sister called us through to the dining room, I tried to catch Lindsay's eye and she smiled, giving nothing away.

I felt a bit numb. I had no idea whether Lindsay had told her, or whether there was about to be an awful scene.

"You're going to be an uncle," Lindsay's sister told her husband as he was sitting, catching him off guard.

"Oh, right, congratulations," he said, coolly, probably wondering why the hell I hadn't mentioned that instead of rambling on about Manchester United's shit defence. I wondered the same thing.

Back in the car, the relief was clear. The hardest part had been done, and her sister had dealt with the news brilliantly – whoever else we told, it would be a piece of piss. Yeah, right.

The next people to hear the news were Lindsay's parents, who'd been looking after the house and pets for us. We'd thought carefully about this one, and planned a little scenario in which we presented her dad with a flat cap – a symbol of his imminent grandpa status – as a souvenir of our trip. We stood back and awaited their response.

His broad smile hid the hurt look in his eyes as he laid the present to one side, doubtless wondering why we were being so rude after he'd given a week of his life to look after our pets.

A few moments later the dull spark that we'd been helplessly fanning in his direction caught Lindsay's mother instead. "You mean you're pregnant?" she whooped, as we breathed sighs of relief and nodded sheepishly. Then the shocked congratulations came flooding out and he beamed with genuine delight.

After all that self-inflicted torture, I decided to just ring my parents to break the news – needless to say it was one hell of a lot easier.

Chapter Two
Senses Working Overtime

All of Lindsay's holiday ailments checked out as normal for early pregnancy during today's visit to the doctor. I was crapping myself about this visit, I'd cleared the morning in case tests and examinations went on for some time and we arrived early, in order to appear keen.

Why the hell did we bother? It was all over in five minutes. So what did I expect? Well, I'd pictured some kind of confirmation – the doctor is meant to be a kindly old guy who leans across his huge oak desk, shakes me warmly by the hand and says 'congratulations, Mr Giles, you're going to be a father'.

Yet our GP ignored this practised etiquette. Firstly she was a woman and secondly she just accepted our positive test as evidence. She didn't even congratulate me. No handshake, nothing. She just asked a few questions, checked blood pressure, examined Lindsay and gave a short lecture on dietary dos and don'ts. We were given a form to fill in, which registers Lindsay for antenatal care, and sent packing. We stood at the reception desk mystified and gutted, looking like a couple who've just had some really bad news.

It's made the whole experience seem even less real than it was before. All we have is a positive pregnancy test – actually we've now done three positive pregnancy tests, just to be certain – and the medical profession are offering nothing more than the promise of a trip to the midwife in a month or so. What the hell am I supposed to do while we wait? What if I do something horribly wrong? Should I force Lindsay to stay indoors, in bed, until it's all over?

Have we been short-changed? Even our parents – during the now daily phone calls – seemed upset that we didn't have more to tell them after this appointment, and they must have been through the same thing.

These frequent parental phone calls follow a dull and consistent pattern. After a brief and insincere enquiry about my health, my mum/ her mum/ her sister asks to speak to Lindsay, desperate to listen to the tiniest detail about her physical well-being. Only half a dozen people know that Lindsay is pregnant, yet they've already managed to make me feel like a complete outsider. And that's just the women – I haven't even spoken to my dad yet, but Lindsay's dad already has the air of someone who expects his son-in-law to get a proper job, shave regularly and start looking after his little girl and, more importantly, his first grandchild.

I'm feeling a bit jealous, to tell the truth. I really don't see why this pregnancy is only seen as Lindsay's achievement. There was a lot of hard work on my part too. Well, a bit. The phrase 'we're pregnant' has always struck horror into my heart, mainly because it sounds like a line from one of those American made for TV movies and it also seems to demonstrate an ignorance of biological fact. But I can understand it a little better now. For better or worse I am a part of this experience, though right now it feels as if I'm a spare part.

· · ·

The doctor estimated that Lindsay is just seven weeks pregnant, so I assumed I wouldn't be thinking about the reality of parenthood for a while. Wrong. Today, a few short days after seeing the doctor, I have been wandering round a nightmarish shopping mall, examining prams, cots, baby gyms and other items too expensive to mention.

Shopping is never my idea of fun, but something was different about the place today, something really creepy. I saw families everywhere – toddlers wandering aimlessly, babies screaming, little hands pulling at trouser-legs, pleading for the ice cream or the toy. There seemed to be, quite literally, kids all over the shop.

Children need a stack of stuff – bow-legged parents were laden like Sherpas with backpacks, pushchairs were weighted down with suspicious looking sacks of utensils and other shit. I wondered how these people expected to actually cram any shopping into their cars.

The answer was crushingly simple – they didn't buy anything. They walked around, occasionally stopping to reach into the undercarriage of the buggy for a camping stool or tyre lever, then wandered on. Sure, they might pick up a paper, or a new pair of bootees, but in reality this was just a day out. Shit. Is this what fatherhood makes of you? If so, I'm in a nightmare.

We haven't even started to tot up the cost of having a child and I wandered open mouthed around a dizzying array of equipment. This was the ultimate contrast to just a few days ago, when the news seemed so incredible, and our lives were so special. In this mall we were surrounded by other couples, some just looking, like us, and some actually buying the contents of their nursery. A dozen women puffed and winced, hands resting on the small of their backs as babies shifted.

We stuck at it for a while, prodding and poking at buggies and travel systems, mentally calculating a rough total of pre-birth spending. But we didn't last long. I couldn't avoid feeling that my unique experience has been violated by a commercial world that isn't merely geared up for pregnancy, it is honed to a complacent perfection.

There are fathers-to-be everywhere and I am just another statistic in a mechanical and predictable business.

How *much*?
Keeping a lid on shopping

A surefire way of sending yourself crazy is to believe all the statistics that tell you babies cost a fortune. The subject of baby accessories is one of those rare areas where it pays to listen to your parents, who will doubtless have stories about how you slept in a milk crate until you were two.

Don't stress about it, babies are cheap – they are flexible, adaptable and not fashion conscious. It is new parents who are expensive – especially those who salivate over all-terrain cots in parenting magazines. Peer pressure is a terrible thing, and when it comes to buying baby accessories there's a strong desire to get the best of everything because it shows your good intentions as a father. But that's advertising for you.

When you do eventually get round to buying the stuff, the trick is to make most of the big decisions together – and I'm talking cot/crib, pram, car seat – so if one of you gets overexcited by the Gucci swing, the other one is there to surgically remove the credit card.

It is the start of week nine and Lindsay's appetite has dropped off to such an extent that, as we both still always cook for two, I am now beginning to show. Pretty soon I'll need a whole new wardrobe.

The things we eat are changing, too – out goes the delicious fresh baked bread and the strong curries, the red wine and red meat. In comes bland chicken and fish and lots of fancy soft drinks made out of Elderflower and Ginseng and other compost heap crap.

None of this is to do with appetite, more with Lindsay's morning sickness, or more correctly her all day sickness. She doesn't have it too bad by all accounts – she's not actually throwing up – but she has a strong and constant reaction to certain smells and I'm trying to sympathise – so despite my reluctance, I'm phasing out the wine for a while. I yearn for a nice rare steak washed down with a couple of bottles of red, but I'm forcing myself to make do with sucking on a carrot and sipping flower juice. It does work for the sickness though, because I'm totally sick of the whole thing. To be fair to Lindsay, she does seem to miss those luxuries too – I just hope this doesn't go on for the whole pregnancy.

"Should I hold your hair?"
Helping her through morning sickness

It's been said that the only thing all women have in common is their unpredictability. Well, the same is true for pregnancy symptoms. Try to second-guess them, and you're stuffed. She looks OK, she seems OK, but then suddenly you're in the middle of a scene from *The Exorcist*.

Morning sickness can, amazingly, be a sickness that affects a woman in the morning. But it can also be a slight nausea that lasts all day, or a large scale vomit fest that only happens in aisle 5 of the supermarket. It's normally a symptom of early pregnancy, and usually fades away by about 12 to 14 weeks. It might be triggered at mealtimes, and by specific smells or tastes. Generally, her senses are heightened, so any strong or distinctive smell may have the potential to cause an extreme reaction.

Some women don't get sick at all, but some can continue to be ill for the whole shooting match. So how do you help her deal with it? The women who wake up, throw up and get on with the day actually seem to get off fairly light, as most of them appear to feel fine thereafter. There's not much you can do for them, except hold the toilet seat.

Lindsay's was a fairly mild but constant illness between about four and 10 weeks. She felt alright most of the time. But when she felt bad, she shied away from food, and that isn't really the best option – eating and drinking little and often is a good answer with these milder symptoms. Get your partner to keep a few biscuits handy – ginger ones in particular seem to work well for many women.

I should have seen the warnings. Today began as grey, chilly and uninviting as any Monday morning in history. I find it pretty hard to get up most days, but something about this morning was saying 'stay where you are'. Normally I need around half a dozen nudges to rouse and then a few flicks of the bedroom light to keep me awake. Even then, I generally drift off again until Lindsay returns from the bathroom and starts crashing around, getting dressed.

This morning I went back to sleep and woke a few minutes later to see Lindsay standing at the bedroom door. As my eyes slowly focused, I noticed that she looked troubled.

"What?" I mumbled.

"I don't know," she said, full of thought. "It's probably nothing, but…well I'm bleeding quite a bit."

I sat up, very much awake. Even in a time of crisis I was keen to show off my new found knowledge on conditions in pregnancy. A discharge of mucky brown blood is a fairly normal thing, fresh blood can mean danger. I've read the books, I could deal with this. "Fresh blood?" I asked.

"A little bit."

"Oh shit. Oh shit, oh shit."

OK, I couldn't deal with this. In fact I was panicking. We dressed and went downstairs. I managed to make a cup of tea and she flicked through the baby books again, looking for something to put our minds at ease.

Though it made me feel horribly guilty to do so, I couldn't help thinking of the worst case, the prospect that she might lose the baby. Lindsay has always been healthy – that must count for something?

Bollocks does it. All of the books I've read and all the people I've spoken to tell me the same thing – miscarriage is a hard, painful and often unbearable fact of life. The books offer as a crumb of comfort the suggestion that it is sometimes nature's way of ending a pregnancy that wasn't going to result in a healthy child, or one that might have harmed the mother. We're talking a very small crumb, here. All the experts agree that once the symptoms begin to show in detail, there is nothing to be done except to get into hospital and let fate take its course.

Facing a nightmare
The threat of miscarriage

No one wants to think about miscarriage. I started out with the attitude that knowing all about it would somehow make the possibility more real. If I shut it out, it couldn't happen to us. But that's total crap. Forewarned is forearmed, so, like it or not – and I know that you don't – here are some stark facts on miscarriage from The Miscarriage Association, a support group helping people through this dreadful experience:

More than one in five pregnancies ends in miscarriage – around a quarter of a million in the UK each year.

Most miscarriages happen in the first three months of pregnancy – but they can happen up to the 24th week. Pregnancy loss after 24 weeks is known as stillbirth.

Any woman who is at risk of pregnancy is also at risk of miscarriage.

Most women never know what has caused them to miscarry. Investigations are generally limited to women who have had three or more miscarriages. Even after investigations, in many cases a specific cause is not found.

But:

Even after several miscarriages, most women have a good chance of a successful pregnancy.

Lindsay went to the bathroom again, and returned with her eyes wet with tears. She was still bleeding. I scoured the books, desperate to find something. But I was never going to find what I was searching for. Nowhere did they tell me how to comfort my fearful wife, nor how to calm the rising nausea in my own gut. What they said, simply and correctly, was that I was helpless.

Lindsay was becoming increasingly distressed. I tried to calm her by explaining that she didn't have certain symptoms. There were no cramps, no pains. Were there? By then anything was possible, she was feeling her worst fears. She was so scared, she didn't know what was symptom and what was imagination.

I felt the cold sweat on my back. I had to take the initiative. I suggested we call the doctors' surgery. There was no reply. We tried NHS Direct. A response, a return call and some reassurance. But the nurse on the phone couldn't see Lindsay, or give any real advice from such a distance. She said we should contact the hospital.

That made it much more real. All of a sudden, we were in an emergency. We called the midwives' out of hours number and were given another number for the hospital's early pregnancy clinic. We called this and arranged to go straight in for a scan.

Hospitals for me have always been places for getting bad news.

They are where people die, or are seriously ill. I couldn't link this place with anything positive. I smiled, I encouraged, I held Lindsay tight as we wandered through the unfamiliar corridors, but I feared the worst.

By the time we reached the waiting room, my stomach was in knots. I had no idea how Lindsay was feeling, all I could see was her vacant, defeated expression. A nurse spoke to us and left us with a form to fill. The NHS' reputation for pointless bureaucracy is undeserved – this form was great therapy, I couldn't ever remember being so happy to focus on the dull details of name and address.

We sat for an age below a TV playing a chat show with the mute button on, flicking blindly through old magazines, hugging each other while our minds raced through all the possibilities.

"Lindsay Giles," a voice called, finally.

I was expecting another of those scenes that TV and film have turned to cliché. But the ultrasound room was a million miles from the huge, clinically white chamber of technology that American film producers can afford. It was small, dark and shabby with the bright light of day framing an ill-fitting curtain at the far end. It was more 'ooh-arr' than ER.

This was one anticlimax we didn't give a stuff about. We could have been sat on orange boxes as long as this scan worked out OK.

The ultrasound operator was a challenge. She sighed deeply as we admitted we hadn't read the information notice on the wall of the waiting room. No shit, lady, we had other things on our minds. Lindsay had to be sent off to empty her bladder before the internal scan could be attempted.

Eventually, we got started. It took a few moments to adjust my eyes to what I was seeing on the monitor. I didn't know whether I was looking for a problem or a baby. The screen showed something that looked like the inside of a football and right in the heart of it was a bean shaped blob. No, not a blob. A really clear, albeit tiny, baby. My baby. OK, our baby.

The operator clicked a few buttons and made some measurements, but said nothing. I began to worry that she hadn't spotted it, or even more worryingly, that I'd mistaken some essential organ for my kid.

I smiled and squeezed Lindsay's hand and she squeezed back, but she couldn't take her eyes off the screen. Eventually, after what felt like several hours, the operator spoke.

"So there's baby," she said. "Looking fine."

Fine. Oh yeah, right. Like this was just something she does every day. Well, OK, so it is. But the matter of fact attitude, the certainty of her description clashed so heavily with our fear of a few minutes earlier.

"But, but the bleeding…?" I stammered.

"Doesn't look like anything to worry about, I'll get doctor to speak to you," she replied. "Congratulations," she said, an insincere afterthought.

And we were out in the waiting room again, blinking in the light, trying to take in what we had just seen as we were sent to another area to wait for the doctor. Eventually he poked his head around the door. "How are you doing?" he asked.

"Fine," we lied.

"Great, I'm a bit tied up, but I'll make sure someone comes and sees you soon," he said. His head disappeared, then returned. "You do know it's good news, right?" he asked.

We nodded vaguely. No, we didn't know it was good news. They seemed to think we were looking for confirmation of the pregnancy, while we wanted to know the cause of the bleeding. In their haste to give us what they thought we wanted, they'd avoided the real issue.

A Sister arrived and finally put our minds at rest. No, the bleeding wasn't strictly 'normal' but it sometimes happened around this time. She explained that some women bleed a little all the way through pregnancy. I couldn't face one more morning like the one we've been through, let alone a few months' worth.

Ultimately, though, I feel reassured. The scan has given no cause for concern. And I have seen our child for the first time – a little jumping bean with stubby arms and legs. When she'd finished grumbling, the ultrasound operator actually pointed out the heart beating.

As emotional rollercoasters go, it doesn't get much more extreme. I am so relieved we've ended it on a high. But it has shown me exactly how underprepared I am for the emotional side of this pregnancy.

Any partner in the situation I've just endured wants to be able to provide the answers to all the worst fears. But short of a few years' medical training and a home ultrasound machine, I'm not going to provide much in the way of concrete help.

"And it comes out of *there*?"
Knowing the medical basics

No, you can't provide concrete help, unless you happen to be an obstetrician, and no, you shouldn't beat yourself up over this fact. Being told about bloody discharges and plugs of mucus isn't necessarily every man's cup of tea. Should you have to embrace every one of your partner's bodily functions? I should damn well hope not. The symptoms of pregnancy can be graphic and disgusting. You don't need to explore them all to show your commitment.

It's a good idea to have a vague understanding of what's happening to her so you can offer support when it really counts, but if you'd rather leave the medical stuff to the professionals, no one should blame you in the slightest. A basic pregnancy book should give you all the information you need to know – though steer clear of the ones with loads of illustrations. On the plus side these have lots of photos of naked women, but on the minus side, they have fewer words and are often, therefore, shit.

What I can improve is the emotional support. That isn't easy when you're every bit as petrified as the person you love. The trick is to have prepared responses and reassurances for any emergency situation, to appear cool, calm and in control. I hadn't wanted to contemplate this situation, but I know I need to plan for the worst and hope for the best. Life will undoubtedly plonk me somewhere in between.

•   •   •

The scare has shaken us both. The excitement of seeing the baby at nine weeks should have been overwhelming, but instead we have become really cautious. The problem with that, of course, is that caution is a constant reminder of the possibility of miscarriage. That's a big burden.

Not looking at clothes or toys, not telling any more people about the pregnancy, not buying anything for the baby, not having sex because of the likelihood of more bleeds, all this implicitly states that we fear losing the baby. It would be better to be endlessly optimistic. But then what is sensible and what is human can be very different things.

Exploding a myth
Sex and miscarriage

There is no link at all between sex in pregnancy and miscarriage. In fact, sex will not harm or endanger the baby at any stage of the pregnancy. But if your partner bleeds in early pregnancy, you might want to avoid penetrative sex for a while, as it can be painful, stressful and not particularly sexy.

I know I'm making the situation worse by worrying all the time. Whenever Lindsay comes back from the bathroom I fire a quick 'alright?' at her. I'm treating her as if she is incredibly fragile, as if the scan has given us cause to worry, rather than be comforted. I've started dithering over decisions, wanting to defer them to the 12 week mark, when the risk of miscarriage begins to reduce. I imagine it as some kind of secure barrier that will make me feel so much better in myself. I can't wait for it to arrive.

• • •

Perhaps the best way to avoid the stress of worrying about miscarriage is to get wrapped up in other things. Week 11 has arrived, and that means a visit to the midwife for Lindsay's booking in appointment.

The midwife is the greatest cliché in my mind. I talked to my parents about their experiences and this has hardened my prejudice, as they assured me that midwives are generally fierce, never sympathetic and always ancient. I already have a mental picture of a fire breathing, starched uniform wearing octogenarian who suspects that any father attending an appointment is a worthless, communist layabout.

After meeting her, I'd like to say that I was absolutely right on all counts. But the midwife is none of the above. She is close to retirement age, but that has only increased my faith in her experience.

She didn't seem to view me with any suspicion. In fact, she barely viewed me at all in the appointment, preferring to devote her focused attention to Lindsay. This is something I understand, expect even, but don't appreciate. There would be uproar if it was suggested that all mothers-to-be should be treated the same. But fathers can, it seems, take what they get and be grateful. I got the chance to ask a few questions and occasionally I got answers as well. But generally I was left with the feeling that I was taking up valuable chair space.

It isn't the first – and I'm sure it won't be the last – time that spare part feeling surfaces in this pregnancy. I want to be there for every push and prod, every puff and blow. The only person who has a similar commitment to stick by Lindsay is the midwife, and this one doesn't seem to welcome my presence. So we are rivals, enemies. This is a battle of wills I am determined to win.

The more I was sidelined by the midwife, the more I cut in; the less my opinion was sought, the more it was offered. Poor Lindsay must have felt like the net judge at Wimbledon, mediating a rally between us. By the end of the appointment I felt as if I'd established a firm position. This woman might not remember my name, but she knows I am serious.

Lindsay gave me an odd look as we walked to the car. I asked her what was wrong. "You're so funny, asking all those questions," she said. I don't think she minds but it would be stretching it to say she is impressed. I think she's surprised and probably quite amused. I hope she is comforted, I take an interest because I want to be involved, but also because I want her to be assured that I am fighting for her. I guess it comes back to the feeling of powerlessness in the scan room.

Not seen and not heard
Trying to deal with the midwife

Good, bad or indifferent, the midwife is the closest thing you will have to a guide in pregnancy, and while your partner may come to rely on her, you might find yourself feeling edged out. It's your responsibility to change that; she will just do her job – and that means she'll focus entirely on your partner's needs.

As the appointments generally involved blood pressure monitoring and, later, heartbeat checks etc, Lindsay was often absorbed by being prodded and poked and forgot to ask the questions we wanted answered. So I'd make sure we talked about it first, then asked those questions myself.

I found that once you've established eye contact with a midwife, you can then start to work on a relationship. Ten, 11, 12 months later, our midwife still didn't know my name, or what I did for a living, but she respected my right to be there.

Arguably the most exciting result of this appointment was the huge folder of leaflets, books and other stuff that Lindsay has been given. We took them home and laughed at the efforts rival baby product firms are prepared to make to secure a share of our funds.

One of the most shameless is a book called 'Emma's Diary' in which Emma details her experiences along with those of her friends from a broad ethnic, cultural and class background. It's terrible. Some effort has been put in to offer a broad sweep of experience, but it's obviously written with an agenda – the poor friend with a bun in the oven and no ring on her finger is beset by endless crises, while Tom and Katy Middle-Class (not their real names) take a couple of hours out from their busy middle management lives to have a baby whose shit doesn't stink. I pity poor Emma for having friends like these, but my real sympathy is reserved for the millions of mothers-to-be who are expected to read this garbage.

Much more worthwhile was the collection of vouchers entitling us to a variety of free samples, gift packs and other goodies which gave us an excuse to hit the shops again. So now, at the end of the day, we have a couple of carrier bags full of stuff. More research is needed, on my part at least, to determine what the hell half the things we've been given are used for. But it's good to know that we have all the nipple cream we can eat.

· · ·

The 12 week landmark has crept up on us. It's changed nothing, I am still jittery about the idea of making concrete plans and we are both wary of the occasional bleeds that Lindsay is having.

Twelve weeks does mark something, however. After our awkward and frankly crap efforts to tell our families about our good news, we have decided to inform friends and colleagues.

This isn't going to be easy, either. Families learn to be tactful over the years. Their instincts are based on the fact that they love you and they are pleased at any good news you have to offer. The same is partly true for friends – good friends anyway – but colleagues aren't required to be delighted for you. I can't help but feel that the reality of life post-baby is about to kick in.

Lindsay has it the hardest. Working in engineering, she faces a fair degree of prejudice from day to day anyway. Now she's got to cope with men saying 'I wondered when that was going to happen' when she breaks the news, as if pregnancy was some kind of character flaw. Many of them will make the false assumption that this is the end of her working life.

Colleagues aren't such an issue when you work for yourself, but I'm still nervous about telling my friends. Fears about loss of youth and independence resurface, especially as our current plan is for me to take on the lion's share of looking after the kid with Lindsay going back to work part time.

I can just imagine what my mates will say about me becoming that dreaded thing 'the househusband'. Actually, they probably won't care, most of them think I spend my days sitting in front of the TV as it is.

Richard and Judy and you?
Being a stay at home dad

The birth of a child is actually the life changing experience everyone claims – so it's also the perfect chance to change a few other aspects of life too. It's why so many people move house with a baby on the way. A recent survey of new fathers showed that more than 40 per cent would like to stay at home with their child. Yet only a small percentage of these men actually go on to achieve that ambition. Why?

Reasons are partly social, partly economic. The man is still seen as the main wage earner, the woman as the best carer. But the world is shifting, and the community of stay at home dads is strengthening all the time. Support networks and online communities exist to help men cope with some of the crap they encounter when making this brave decision.

It's a complex issue, and one that is addressed fully in Richard Hallows' *Full Time Father* (White Ladder), but the basic pros and cons are straightforward. If you don't mind your own company and you're happy watching daytime TV while ironing baby clothes or cleaning up milk vomit then you've got what it takes. If you want an unrepeatable chance to bond with your child and discover your own resourcefulness, then you really should consider it.

In fact, what worries me more is the fear that I'll give up being my old self after this kid arrives. I want to feel reassured by the strength of my own convictions – the belief that I will somehow succeed in juggling my work and childcare in spite of the obvious strain it'll put on my time management skills.

Rather than waste time contacting everyone, I simply broke the news to an old journalism colleague of mine. Sure enough the news spread fast. Within hours of our boozy lunch, half a dozen friends got in touch to check, partly tongue in cheek, whether this new arrival would be the end of my 'career' ambitions. Right now it's hard to believe that it isn't.

Chapter Three
Slave to Love

While I've been worrying about the future, Lindsay has been getting on with the present. The sickness has subsided and her appetite is slowly returning, but she still reacts to some smells and tastes. By far the worst symptom is tiredness. She struggles through the day with barely enough energy to make it home. Her evenings are short and uneventful, her nights long and uncomfortable.

Tiredness is a common symptom, but normally from about 14 weeks things start to become a little easier, and it's when most women regain some of their zest for life. It's a landmark I can't wait to see for one particular, selfish reason. Lindsay has always needed her full eight hours' sleep, but she is starting to drag herself off to bed at nine. We aren't seeing much of each other. In other words, I'm starting to fret about sex.

I'm not one of those men who insists on his conjugal rights every Saturday night in the gap between Casualty and Match of the Day. But it's been a couple of weeks now, and I'm starting to think about the prospect of longer term celibacy.

Far be it from me to use the old gag about sex being all ups and downs, but it does seem to be a case of feast followed by famine. Not that I'm being starved; if anything I'm the one holding back. Frankly, I haven't worked out a strategy for approaching sex in this pregnancy. Do I assume things will carry on as normal? Do I change my attitude about what is expected of me in bed? Or do I resort to a helping hand in the time honoured spirit of Do It Yourself?

Five finger exercise
Satisfying yourself

The fact that I'm scratching around for a euphemism for masturbation suggests that it is still very much a taboo subject. And I believe it is. Which is very bad news for most pregnant fathers, who will either have to learn extreme self-control or the ability to have a quick one off the wrist without feeling like a naughty schoolboy. Most men I know masturbate well beyond their teenage years, though only a few of them are honest about it. I'm not suggesting it's something to bring up at dinner parties, but it is a very useful, safe and acceptable weapon in your war against sexual frustration. So use it. But don't wear it out.

The answer, of course, is all of the above. I'm only going to get through this most personal and awkward part of the process by attending to my own basic needs, trying to find out what Lindsay is happy and comfortable with and learning to cope with a lower position in the pecker, sorry, pecking order than before. I mean, sod it, it's only short term. Isn't it?

Habits, tricks and bigger tits
Sex in pregnancy (part one)

The subject of sex throws up a couple of other pitfalls for the pregnant father. First is the less common but equally genuine concern that the woman develops a really strong sex drive and the man goes off sex altogether – possibly because of worry about harming the baby, or because he finds his partner less attractive.

It's hard to deal with this without hurting your partner's feelings, but deal with it you must – if she is craving attention and you're not giving it there'll be real problems ahead. It doesn't mean you have to turn into a shag monster against your will, just reassure her that you are as loving and attentive as you were before – simply by giving her more hugs and affection or maybe by satisfying her without penetrative sex. Unfortunately, giving oral sex isn't always easy for men in pregnancy: some women experience fairly strong smelling discharges that can be pretty off-putting. It might be time to read that sensual massage book and try out a few new moves.

The second major issue in the bedroom is the tricky matter of her tits. They are going to get bigger, which, on the face of it, seems like a bonus just for you. But the flip side is that suddenly they don't seem to be your playthings after all. It's an immediate, blunt welcome to the world beyond your neat little pairing. There is now a third party involved, and your partner's body is changing to accommodate that involvement.

As with all these issues of sex, sensitivity is the key, so don't start to think of her tits as a feeding station as your partner won't thank you for the dehumanising effect of this – she'll already be feeling like some kind of alien 'host'. Treat her tits with the respect that engorged, sore and sensitive body parts deserve, but don't let that put you off.

One thing I know for sure, doing without sex is better than pestering her all the time. She has started to be afflicted by minor mood swings, which added to the nausea and tiredness, means she's not necessarily attached to my genitalia at present. I would like to stay attached to them, so I'll keep a low profile.

"Where did I leave those scissors?"
Coping with mood swings

If you thought that hormones just do strange physical things to your partner, you should try watching a soppy film with her. Lindsay would weep buckets at a slightly gloomy weather report and would howl with sympathy whenever Tom failed to catch Jerry. OK, that's a slight exaggeration, but her moods did begin to swing, albeit gently, with a fair degree of regularity.

It seems that few women are really moody during pregnancy, their emotions – like their senses – are often just heightened. So the old cliché about pregnant women flying off the handle at the slightest thing is mainly pub banter. If you behave as you normally would, but with a greater degree of sensitivity, you'll probably avoid too much hassle. So don't forget birthdays, anniversaries and special occasions, don't make more work for your partner around the house, don't tell her you're thinking of giving up work and driving round Europe on a Harley.

It might help to think of moodiness as a symptom of pregnancy, rather like morning sickness. When she started throwing up or feeling ill, your first thought wasn't 'oh no, she's going to be like this every day for the rest of our lives,' was it? So if she snaps a bit now and then, smile, apologise and put it down to the miracle of childbearing. Making a big issue out of it won't solve anything, and you'll have to back down anyway. So be wise, philosophise and this too shall pass.

On the subject of profile, until now Lindsay's parents have been keeping theirs high, keen to show that they are interested, informed and in my face. They call frequently with wise counsel on a variety of subjects, mainly diet and exercise. Had the advice been invited, it would be welcome, but I know that their ideas on childcare belong with Spangles and Tartan trousers in the mid-Seventies.

I also know that they mean well, but I take their advice as seriously as that of my grandmother, who campaigns for Guinness to be made available on prescription. According to her, a bottle a day is Lindsay's answer. It would take at least that for her to be able to cope with the quick-fire questioning of her parents.

The worst part – and they are not the only relations or friends guilty of this – is that although I'm happy to field all their questions, they don't seem to believe I could possibly know anything about the pregnancy. It is a very patronising attitude, and it makes me feel like shit. Months before antenatal classes, I'm getting lots of early practice at deep breathing techniques.

"And another thing..."
Dealing with unwanted opinions

Pregnancy can make you feel a bit like you're under attack, even if everything's going smoothly. If your partner is having a rough time of it, there will be a million different opinions blasting at her from relatives and well-wishers. Your role here is intervention and information management. Help her sift the good intentions from the crap, and then keep the crap at bay. There's nothing more upsetting than some dried up old spinster of a great aunt going on about how eating apples in pregnancy causes typhoid.

So don't be afraid to act tough. Setting the parameters of acceptable behaviour now means that when the baby is born people will respect your privacy that much more. Right now you're probably being patronised by mothers who think they know better, and bizarrely by fathers as well, but don't let them wind you up – this is your show and you can run it any way that makes you and your partner comfortable.

My parents don't bombard us with questions, but they have done something that threw me right off track. They came over for lunch yesterday – Mothers' Day – and brought Lindsay a present. It was so strange, I couldn't get my head around the idea that she is going to be a mother. It sounds so grown-up. We will be parents, I will be a father, and soon. None of this should come as much of a surprise to me, but I hadn't put it in context, I'm so wrapped up in the idea of the pregnancy that I haven't thought much about the end prod-

uct. It's also weird that this revelation should come from my parents – suddenly we are going to be placed on an equal footing with
them, all parents together. It feels like a massive and immediate
leap into some kind of secret society and I'm not yet sure I'm comfortable with it.

•　　•　　•

Because of the emergency scan after nine weeks, the hospital decided not to do a 12 week scan. We talked this over with the midwife
and she agreed that we should get a scan done after all. Actually she
said something along the lines of 'this is your baby and you need to
get what you can. Be selfish, put yourselves first'. This isn't great
advice, too much of that sort of crap just screws everything up for
everyone. But we've already sussed that in the harsh world of free
healthcare, those who keep silent are dumb. Anyhow, we don't
want the Earth, just the chance to renew contact with that jumping bean.

So today we were back in the hospital, in the same area where we'd
sat and imagined the unimaginable. This time we were totally different people, we followed the instructions carefully, beamed joy-
ously at the surly attendants and sat enchanted as the operator
made sense of the shadows and patterns on the screen. It was quite
frustrating to watch the scan, which was of the traditional, gel on
the belly type. It was fuzzier and less conclusive than the internal
nine week job.

The operator was pointing out the baby lying at the bottom of the
screen when suddenly it gave a terrific jump, perfectly in the
centre of the shot, did a backflip and waved at us. OK, so I made
up those last two, but it definitely jumped, a magnificent leap that
was captured for ever, as the operator printed off a still for us to
keep.

The picture is a big bonus. The people in the ultrasound unit recommended that we shouldn't try to get pictures until 20 weeks, but this gives us something real to hang on to. I don't care that my child now resembles a misshapen monkey nut, I love it, and, assuming it won't actually stay like that, I know I'll look back with great affection on this early snapshot.

Lindsay feels the same, only more so. When we got back from the appointment, she raced to the scanner and computer and produced an assortment of copies, enlargements, reductions, T-shirts and posters. If a mother's love for her child can be measured out in ink and paper, then our baby has a bright future. We now have more pictures of our 12 week old foetus than we do of each other after eight years together.

The measurements taken by the ultrasound operator match the estimated due date calculated at the doctor's, meaning that our child was almost certainly conceived during that drunken anniversary celebration. I feel a bit guilty at the thought of a new life springing from so much alcohol, but at least it was a happy start to life.

•   •   •

The pace of life in general seems to have taken over, the only evidence of the pregnancy are baby magazines and clothing catalogues littering our lounge. And I mean littering. Lindsay's general lethargy keeps her from doing much around the house and I'm worried that if I start doing the housework I'll be given the job permanently.

I don't want to sell myself short here, there are things I'm good at – washing up is one of my specialities. I can also vacuum pretty well. But I'm like a high class cleaning prostitute, I have my boundaries. I don't dust, I don't iron, I don't do French. No aprons.

And yet, some of this stuff simply has to be done. Washing, for example, is a disputed territory, as is cooking. Both seem to be essential, but does that mean I have to take the initiative? Probably. If you weigh up the pros and cons, all I have on my side is the fact that I'm crap at these things, while Lindsay has all the emotional strings, like needing a good diet and clean clothes for work. I feel abused, but I don't think there's much mileage in complaining.

"How long do you boil lettuce?"
Your role as hired slave

It may feel that the moment you learned your partner was pregnant you signed an unwritten contract to become her hired slave. To a certain extent that's true – there are many things that she will be unable or unwilling to do in her pregnant state that must be picked up by other people and relieving the pressure of chores and similar stresses is probably your largest responsibility this side of labour. But that doesn't mean you have to do it all – it might mean project managing a team of willing and non-judgmental relatives to help with ironing, cooking, cleaning etc. If you can afford it, you could also consider getting some paid help – it won't be for long, and sending out your ironing instead of sweating over it all evening is well worth the price of a takeaway.

Cooking is a real problem, made worse by the fact that it has become a battle of wills. Lindsay's appetite is still poor, and she would skip meals if it was left to her – but I keep badgering her, offering a banana here, a cheese sandwich there. I struggle to find new ways to present boiled vegetables, and with summer coming I know I'll be just as limp with salad.

A few days ago I thought I had it cracked, thanks to my new friend the dried apricot. According to food experts, this wrinkled morsel of rubbery gunk is the answer to all our prayers. One small portion boosts Lindsay's diet and saves me from being creative. This flaw-less plan – involving a quick trip to the supermarket where I cleared the shelf of dried apricots – fell apart when Lindsay got sick of the damned fruit after the first bag.

•   •   •

Fortunately, as so often happens in life, fate has saved me from making an even bigger arse of myself. Lindsay's zest has returned. Well, maybe 'zest' is pushing it a bit – she's still tired all the time – but she's taken over in the kitchen again. Apricots are banned.

In my rediscovered free time, I've written a feature for a website on the first few weeks of Lindsay's pregnancy. It's short, and I thought it was just a bit of fun but it has produced a couple of big reactions which stopped me in my tracks.

The first has come from an old boss of mine, a proud and devoted mother. I told her about the feature and she promised to take a look. When I saw her next, she gave me a dark look and shook her head.

"I'm angry with you," she said. "I can't believe you can say this," she added, jabbing at a printout of the feature. She pointed out the section that had upset her, in which I said I 'feel like a louse for inflicting months of discomfort and disruption on someone I love so much'.

She said that no mother would feel that something as special as a baby was a 'disruption'. She might be right. But I was talking about me. Me. It may not have been how the 'burden' of pregnancy is viewed by Lindsay, or by any mother, but it is absolutely true for me. When she saw the baby on the monitor at the hospital for the first time, I'm sure she felt real elation – it probably even surpassed the nausea and tiredness. But I haven't got that attachment, the immediate responsibility that you can only get when something inside you is depending on you for its existence. All I have is love for my wife, and a desire to keep her and the baby secure. If I want to feel like a louse, I'm damned if anyone's going to stop me, because I want to be part of the relationship that is bonding between my wife and our child.

The second response was from a friend in business. His family means everything to him, though he is separated and rarely sees his children.

"I can't believe you've missed the more important part," he spluttered.

I shrugged, lost for words. I couldn't imagine what it was I'd forgotten.

"No mention of the pressure to earn money to support the family?" he said, staring incredulously at me, expecting the realisation to hit me like a wet fish.

"I suppose," I said.

"No suppose about it," he snapped. "It's the single biggest pressure. I used to lie awake at night wondering what would happen if I lost my job. I mean, I used to worry before – but as soon as she was pregnant it all got much more serious." He stopped and thought for a few moments. "But then you just don't have that, do you?"

I smiled, shrugged and changed the subject. But now my mind keeps returning to his comments. Maybe he is right. As Lindsay is the main wage earner, I haven't needed to think too much about it. But in a few months she's going on maternity leave and things are going to get tight. And I haven't even started to think about what happens afterwards.

We've planned things quite well and have a few savings, but any little disaster could throw all that off. We've both been through a fair share of upheaval in our working lives – company closures, redundancies, shit bosses, crap conditions – but we've always come through. Perhaps I just have faith in our ability to make something out of the situation. Perhaps I just haven't given it enough thought. Maybe I do have something to panic about after all.

I've tried to think of friends in similar situations. One of my former colleagues is a single father – he's juggled his full time job with childcare. He's used a nursery and that isn't what we want. So if I do have to start bringing in a more reliable income, it needs to be part time at best.

Another friend runs a business from home, supporting his wife and three children. Here is a success story, a man in complete control of his finances and his relationships. He has the flexibility to adapt to any situation and the money to raise his family.

I liked the sound of this, so I talked to him about the realities of his situation. Sure, he agreed, he has a good balance, and he is rarely short of work. But this is the result of 10 years' grafting. He told me about the early days, the long hours, the lack of sleep, not taking a holiday for fear of losing lucrative work. All the usual pressures that go with starting a business – magnified by the pressure of knowing that you have a child on the way. But, he conceded, life is good now. It has been worth it.

So by the sounds of it I should be in flexible, part time work with a high guaranteed income. But what to choose? Politics, dentistry or royalty? No, all the jobs with large salaries and short hours have been taken.

A return to 'proper' full time work wouldn't ease any worries, except those of our parents, who belong to a generation that mistakenly believes the words Status Quo represent both quality of music and quality of life. We will only be happy if we live life in a way that we can legitimately call our own. I think financial fears are a fact of all our lives, whether we're in control of the purse strings or not. I might not feel the same level of pressure as my breadwinning friend, but that doesn't mean I don't want the best for my family. I'll do what it takes to keep our financial future secure, but I'm not about to start panicking about things I can't control.

• • •

Life has started to speed up worryingly. Weeks are zipping past so quickly that another major milestone has passed us by.

During the booking in appointment, the midwife mentioned a routine, optional procedure of carrying out a blood test for diseases like Spina Bifida and Down's Syndrome at 15 weeks. We'd both shaken our heads at the idea and the suggestion that it carried and I forgot all about it.

But now that 15 weeks have come and gone, we have been reminded, by books rather than the medical profession, that this option had been available. I asked Lindsay how she felt about missing it.

Unlike me, she has been giving it some detailed thought. It's understandable – the responsibility of caring for a disabled child falls on both parents, but if a couple decide to abort a foetus, suddenly the balance swings towards the mother. She has to deny her instincts and agree to the elimination of something with which she has already established a bond.

I don't claim to understand the moral reasons for or against abortion, but I know that if it is thought to be necessary, for medical or social reasons, it could never be seen as an easy option.

For Lindsay, it isn't an option. Which for me is a big relief, because I want us to care for our child whatever. We've both stayed as opposed to testing as we were on that first midwife appointment. I'd say that the decision isn't the important thing, the unity is.

What's going on in there?
Testing for problems

Testing for abnormalities and disabilities is a pretty tough issue, and it's one that you have to get your head around. Whether or not you feel comfortable making the final decision to test or not, you have a right to know the facts of the situation.

Bloods can be taken from around 15 weeks to test for problems like Spina Bifida and Down's. Results are fairly quick in coming, but aren't 100 per cent accurate or conclusive – they just show whether there's an increased likelihood of certain problems. A more precise form of testing is amniocentesis, which is a more complex procedure involving the removal of a sample of amniotic fluid from the uterus. This test gives a truer indication of likely problems, but also carries a tiny risk of miscarriage.

So in a nutshell, the deeper you get into testing, the riskier it is, though it is more likely to prove conclusive. It's an area that needs specialist medical consultation, but that doesn't mean you should just listen to the doctor and ignore your own feelings. Testing isn't about a pregnancy, it's about a child, or even an adult, that you're going to have to help care for. You need to be an informed and willing participant in the decision making process.

Moments like that are cropping up throughout the pregnancy, small yet crucial decisions that may have an impact for years afterwards. I think it is partly why so many men think impending fatherhood makes them grow up suddenly. The truth is, it doesn't make me feel any more adult, just more aware of the consequences of decisions. It makes me think and sometimes it scares me. Sometimes these decisions take a while to be reached, but I try never to avoid them. Well, almost never.

I've taken one decision that I've been putting off from day one. The inevitability is the worst part, the more I have allowed myself to delay, the harder it has become. In the end I have decided simply to face it, even though I could put it off for many more weeks, months even.

Today, I decided to convert the relaxing, crowded, creative sanctuary formerly known as The Study into the soft, fluffy, book free chamber of horrors that is to become The Nursery.

I have worked alone, like a convict cracking rocks. I've bought a pile of cardboard crates, miniature coffins for my effects, and filled them with most of the books, stationery and crap that I've collected over the years.

I am allowed just three five feet bookshelves, moved to a new location in our bedroom, and a small desk. I have spent an unsightly amount of time weighing up which books to take with me to this desert island, repeating the process for CDs, pens, paper and ornaments.

It is pitiful. I have agonised over ring binders and highlighter pens, struggled to squeeze extra books onto my permitted shelving. Even worse than the rationing, working in the bedroom will mean keeping my desk tidy, filing and even, God forbid, throwing things away.

The fact that my little empire can be packed so easily into boxes to make way for the baby raises many questions over my future independence. Is it a sign of things to come? Will any of these boxes see the light of day again, or will they eventually move from loft to dump without another thought. It makes me uneasy. How can I work without my stuff?

Lindsay has clearly entered the unsympathetic phase of pregnancy, pointing out that I have both pen and paper at my disposal, and that my laptop needs very little space as it can, apparently, be operated on my lap. Yes, yes, very funny, but what about my cricket trophy, my hipflask and my hand held paper shredder?

Anyway, back to the decoration of the nursery. As it is replacing my workspace, I've been allowed a bit of freedom over the choice of décor. I've settled on cream for the walls, the door and the ceiling. The floorboards have survived, but they bear many traces of the struggle. The overall effect is, well, cream. It is a blank canvas on which to stamp the individuality of our child. And it has used up all that old cream paint.

Now all we need is a clear idea of our child's gender and a heavy dose of inspiration to create a memorable and attractive room. Both are a long way off. For the time being it is set to stay as a big, off-white, empty shell. I stand in it and remember happy days. I need to get out more.

Chapter Four
Long Hot Summer

Three months ago I didn't even know the baby existed. Now it has its own bedroom, a wardrobe, a crib and a bath. It has a load of prospective babysitters and a whole street of interested well-wishers. And yet it still isn't even halfway to being born. Talk about attention seeking.

Every part of life seems to be about the baby right now. In the last couple of weeks we've enjoyed trips to the midwife for blood pressure checks and a quick listen to the baby's heartbeat, to the obstetrician for a consultation on the back problems that Lindsay has started to experience and to the doctor for another dazzlingly irrelevant session of nervous platitudes.

We've even started renting an allotment so that next year we can grow all the vegetables for the baby's food. There is a good point to this: it is somewhere we can go which doesn't have a baby magazine, a doctor's appointment card or a fluffy toy anywhere in sight. It is a small plot, but it feels like an island, an oasis in the desert of antenatal care. We both get a bit stressed about the fact that babies are apparently the only subject on the minds of parents and siblings, even friends and colleagues. So it's good to have somewhere to slide off to and dig for sanity.

Back to babies. Next week is the 19th of the pregnancy and Lindsay is booked for another session with our old friends in the ultrasound room. It'll be a full six weeks since we saw them and I just know they'll be aching to catch up with us.

This is the anatomy scan, the big one. This is the time when the operator checks for club feet, hare lips, heart and spine problems. All massive, life changing things. We eagerly await confirmation of our baby's good health. But I can't get away from the fact that this is also the moment when we might get an idea of the baby's sex.

Does it really matter? Not particularly. It's possible that the Giles bloodline would die out if we didn't produce a son, and that in turn might mean the sale and dispersal of various family heirlooms – though whether we'd get much more than a fiver for my grandmother's hostess trolley and expanding globe cigarette holder remains to be seen.

I know my grandmother would like a boy, I suspect my mother would like a girl. Lindsay is undecided. I'd just like a baby, though of course I reserve the right to send it back if it starts supporting Manchester United.

It is equally irrelevant to know the baby's gender for financial or practical reasons. There's no harm in waiting to paint that pink or blue mural on the cream study, sorry nursery, wall. The same goes for clothes – white and pastel shades will do just fine for the first few months.

For my money, the only real reason for knowing the baby's gender at this stage is to start bonding. For the last three months we've referred to our baby as 'the blob', which is all well and true to photographic evidence. But nothing inhibits bonding like the belief that you're nurturing something from a 1950s disaster movie.

Speculating means nothing as I've also been warned how difficult it is to prise information about gender from the ultrasound operator. In our age of law suits, hospitals have to be extra careful about telling future parents such things. It's easy to make mistakes, and apart from the practical inconvenience of getting it wrong, there's a real risk of throwing off that bond between child and parents if they don't get what they expect.

So maybe we shouldn't ask. But then, it would be good to know. But then, they won't tell, so then…bugger it, we'll see.

Can you tell what it is yet?
Finding out the gender

Hospitals do seem to be getting the message across that predetermining gender is a risky business. Just 10 percent of the fathers surveyed actively sought to find out the baby's sex early. A couple of the men I spoke to actually felt the bonding issue went the other way: if they were secretly yearning for a boy and discovered early on that it was a girl, they'd worry about feeling a bit less attached to the baby.

It's obviously a personal issue, but if you are desperate to find out and don't want to get the brush off from a lawyer shy hospital you could pay to have a private scan done at a slightly later stage than the traditional 20 week anatomy scan. You'd have a better chance of seeing the business end of the baby clearly and some private clinics have the latest technology which gives a much more realistic image (some even in colour!) than the fuzzy blobs on standard ultrasound kit. It'll cost you, but if you're one of those guys who just can't wait, it might be worth it.

Or not. Another bad day at the ultrasound as our baby flatly refused to behave itself. Everything started so well, I found a parking space in the same health authority as the hospital, walked just half a mile to the department and waited for no longer than the time it takes to Improve Your Word Power in a four year old copy of *Reader's Digest.*

But as soon as we were in and the monitor was switched on, the baby defied all attempts to measure, monitor and observe its behaviour. A fair amount of poking and pummelling later and the only result was that Lindsay's bladder was in serious danger of exploding.

The ultrasound operator gave up in the end, deciding that we need to come back when the baby's in a better position, when it is bigger and when the newer, more powerful ultrasound machine is available.

It's a big anticlimax. Everything about this scan was important to us, and we feel let down by its inconclusive result. After all the fuss over whether we would ask about the gender, I didn't even think to mention it.

•   •   •

Lindsay is now at the halfway stage. In about 20 weeks we will have a baby, a new life, and I will be its father. It is a thought that is immediately humbling, exciting, petrifying and empowering. And I am not remotely ready for it. If I'm going to do the slightest justice to my child, I have to pull myself together now. Time is running out. We've been to stay with my parents for a week – our last holiday before the baby – and that strange feeling I encountered on Mother's Day resurfaced. I've never known them talk so much about their own experiences, I've found out loads of stuff about my childhood that I didn't know, but even more about what my parents were like at our age. It explains a lot and it's one of the most unexpected and rewarding bits of the pregnancy so far.

Meanwhile, it's back to the ultrasound room. We've got back from holiday to find the appointment letter for the rescan, set for the middle of next week, a mere fortnight after the disappointing first effort.

All the hopes and fears from that first anatomy scan have resurfaced. The gender issue has slipped a bit on the order of priorities, the bigger concern now is that everything is where it should be.

•   •   •

This time the baby was in a better mood and a clearer position. We had incredible views of perfect fast bowler's hands and immaculate footballer's feet. We even saw the little symmetrical valves of the heart at work. Everything else seemed to check out.

The only downside of this scan was that it took three times longer than any of the previous ones. Lindsay took a real bruising and at one stage she was sent off to the loo to partially release the pressure on her swollen bladder. Ouch. The old spare part feeling returned with a vengeance as I watched, wincing with sympathetic pain as the operator frantically manipulated Lindsay's bump to try and get a better view.

Once we were done and packed off with yet more photos to add to our burgeoning collection, Lindsay began to feel pretty sick. I wasn't feeling too clever, either.

If I baulk at the sight of Lindsay being gently poked by a kindly lady just doing her job, how the hell am I going to cope with labour? Now that the 20 week mark has passed I can't help thinking that we're counting down to that fateful day.

If my uneducated imagination is anything to go by, she will be rushed in to the hospital ready to pop about 20 minutes after the first contraction. She'll squeeze my hand so tightly it will hurt, she'll call me a worthless bastard, scream and pant a bit, then she'll give birth to a flawless, clean and quiet baby at which stage I'll hand out cigars. Perhaps I can cope with that after all.

●   ●   ●

The midwife – our only friend in the dog eat dog world of antenatal care – had a really bad day today and left us both feeling crap.

First, she again failed to come up with the results of bloods Lindsay gave ages ago, second she failed to find a heartbeat, precipitating more prodding, bruising and bashing for Lindsay. Finally she listened with barely contained awe as Lindsay was forced to explain the finer points of the new maternity rights and demand a form to claim her maternity pay before it is too late. The midwife wandered off to consult with a colleague who was similarly bemused by the changes in mothers' rights, but in the end she gave in, gave us the form and sent us away. Thank God we didn't start on paternity rights.

Get what's coming to you
Paternity pay

Now is a good time to start thinking about paternity leave, which has been improved since new legislation in 2003, but which still won't set your world alight. It's hard to put the complex qualifying conditions in a nutshell, but basically here goes: if you've been employed by a company for at least six months without a break up to the 15th week before the baby's due date, you're probably entitled to a maximum of two weeks' leave on statutory pay. You only get the money if your earnings are above a certain amount (£79 a week gross in April 2004), and the money per week is capped to a maximum (£102.80, April 2004) or 90 per cent of earnings if your pay is less than that figure.

It's not a get rich quick scheme, but it does mean you can get a bit of extra leave without too much financial hardship. You have to tell your employer when you want the leave by the 15th week before the due date (so probably when your partner is 25 weeks approx), and the claim must be made by self-certification – you can get a form from the Inland Revenue. The Revenue and the Department for Work and Pensions provide the most up-to-date information on entitlements and conditions.

It is particularly depressing to be buggered around by her because she has stood alone as the person who claimed to be fighting from our corner. I'm not questioning her professionalism, or the abilities of any of the medical staff we've encountered. But what I'd like is a bit more empathy with the fact that it is all new to us – new and frightening. When something goes wrong, or a test is delayed or overlooked, I'd like to know why, not because I'm pushy, but because it matters.

It might be stupid or naïve to expect to be kept informed and updated at all times – that might be asking too much of a stretched NHS. But in reality all I'm asking is that people who face the process of pregnancy day after day in their working lives acknowledge that we don't. For us this is unique and special, and there's no reason they can't respect that. It costs nothing and it means everything.

• • •

Lindsay is 23 weeks pregnant, she has a bump that would draw admiring glances at the World Darts Championships and the summer has delivered its first heatwave – all of which has contributed to her feeling of discomfort.

The bump hasn't loomed large until now, not because it hasn't been evident, but simply because it isn't something I've thought much about. It has gradually appeared and now it is a part of life, making Lindsay walk a bit oddly, giving her increased difficulty when bending down and picking stuff up. But generally she wears it well. Some men take offence at the shape of the pregnant woman, and I guess I can understand that, it's a part of the realisation that your partner is changing from the girl you know into a mother, maybe even into HER mother. Put it that way and it scares the shit out of me, too. Some men go the other way and find pregnancy a complete turn-on. Though I've never explored this avenue, I'm assured there are even porn magazines devoted to pregnant women. Yes, well.

Lindsay's currently away on a management course. She told me on the phone last night that one of their tasks was to set personal objectives for the next six months. She didn't know whether she should write 'have a baby'.

Life is pretty weird for her right now. She's good at her job in spite of the male environment – mainly because she has been able to be accepted as one of 'the blokes'. But pregnancy changes all that. Some of the men have adapted well, some haven't. They all seem to treat her slightly differently and I think that has unsettled her. Many of her peers are fathers, so they have the advantage of hindsight. Little jibes about forgetfulness and hormones might seem harmless enough, but I can see how much it offends her sense of professionalism. All of a sudden, she's uncertain about who she is.

I feel the same. This short period of total independence is potentially the last time we'll be apart before the baby is born. Approaching these few days, I've had plenty of plans – to lounge around in my underwear, get drunk in the morning, watch a pile of crappy films, write a crappy play – spread out, be selfish, fart a lot and enjoy a last bite of the fruit of hedonistic independent living.

It is now 8pm. Lindsay has called, I've eaten my dinner, washed up and now I'm settling down with a small glass of beer. So far today I've managed to do the washing, the ironing and the vacuuming. I've walked the dogs a few times, posted a letter and had a bath, making sure to clean it thoroughly afterwards. Woah, there. Wild man.

OK, so I'm now a stranger to hedonism. Responsibility creeps up on you from the minute you agree to share a house with someone, for reasons both financial and emotional. If you get a pet, you're tied even more. We have four pets, not counting the livestock in the garden and the mice in the walls. It turns out that I'm already a family man, whether I'm prepared for it or not.

• • •

I am so glad that Lindsay is back from her course. Not just because it means I can stop feeling pressured to do something meaningless and wild in her absence, but because I worry about her every movement. I spend so much time imagining possible problems and traumas that it becomes a great relief to see her fit and well at the end of each day.

And she is well. Not only that, she is blooming. She's decided that she'll take some holiday then start maternity leave early, essentially giving up work at 30 weeks. It's a relief for me, but a bigger one for her — her loyalties have been split between wanting to do a good job and wanting to get on with the whole baby thing.

She gets a pile of e-mails every day from eager baby product manufacturers, trying to impart knowledge and shift a few nappies into the bargain. Each of these has general tips for well-being and a few pointers on what to look out for. My favourite one arrived this morning. It said something along the lines of 'don't be disturbed if your partner starts to behave differently. He may take up a hobby, like woodwork, or grow a moustache'. Come on, you people, how many men have actually responded to the news of impending fatherhood by growing facial hair? And woodwork?

"Darling, I'm pregnant."

"That's wonderful darling. And look, I've made a pipe rack."

"You animal. Come here, I want to feel your stubble against my cheek."

I appreciate the general message that is coming across here – men tend to act more grown-up in response to the approaching demands of fatherhood. Most blokes I know feel they aren't ready for the new arrival, that they still have plenty of growing up to do themselves. That's absolutely understandable and totally human. But woodwork? Moustaches? God no, please don't let it be true.

I should add at this stage that my incredulity bears no relation to the fact that I was kicked out of woodwork at school and have always been cursed with a thin beard. It's just grade A bullshit, pure and simple.

"And we call this a nappy..."
Dealing with stereotypes

It might be bullshit, but it is a symptom of a wider problem that you've probably already started to encounter, and will certainly come up against as the due date approaches. You are about to be stereotyped, bracketed, patronised and condescended to on a scale not seen since you had that maths teacher with B.O. in the third year. It'll come from everywhere – from parents who've done it all, from medical professionals, from books and from TV.

You are a buffoon, a gibbering idiot who forgets to pack the bag, gets lost in the hospital, puts on nappies back to front, passes out in the delivery suite etc, etc. Think of every cliché and comic image of fathers-to-be, and you'll be labelled with almost all in the next couple of months. Is this a bad thing? It depends on your reaction. If it angers you, then it's bad. If you start to believe it, that's a tragedy. But low expectations could give you the space you need to get confident about your role before and after the birth. After all, if everyone's expecting you to fall flat on your face, every little success will feel great.

For the last few weeks Lindsay has been feeling serious movements from the baby. They started about six weeks ago as a fluttering sensation and have been building in intensity ever since. While it was still a novelty, she'd shout to me to come and feel her belly. By the time I got there, the baby was done stretching and had settled back to sleep, or it had shifted sufficiently to start booting her lower spine instead.

Only recently have the kicks been so powerful and frequent that I've been able to feel them too. It's such a weird feeling, and so hard to visualise the little foot or elbow that's stretching Lindsay's skin and fighting for a bit more room inside. In one sense it's great to be able to feel and see the growth of the child, but in another way it also reinforces the fact that I'm just an observer of this curious double act.

Lindsay's even started to detect a pattern of waking and sleeping at fixed times. The baby's most awake at about 3am, but I'm hoping it'll grow out of it. I'm a little jealous of the unmistakeable and unavoidable closeness that's building up between my wife and child.

The other disadvantage of a regular pattern of kicks and punches is that I fly into an immediate panic if Lindsay says the baby has gone quiet. I really should have invested in that portable ultrasound monitor – I bet I could have picked one up on E-Bay.

This happened just yesterday. Lindsay went off to work like normal, but through breakfast, she'd been worried about the fact that she hadn't felt the baby move for a few hours. I wanted her to stay at home, maybe go into the hospital for a scan, but we looked at the books again and they seemed to suggest it wasn't always something to worry about. After about 28 weeks, it ought to be normal to detect around 10 distinct movements every day, but until then the odd lengthy period without a flinch isn't a big worry.

Unfortunately, the downside of working from home is that you've got nothing to distract you from worrying that there is a real problem. With mother and child half an hour away at work, all I could do was sit and fret. Well, that was my excuse for playing computer games all day.

Is there anybody there?
Getting help and guidance

Assuming that you want to avoid being talked down to by smug new fathers – who a few short months ago were crapping themselves in your shoes (as it were) – your options for expressing and discussing your fears are limited. While it's good to talk to your partner, you might want to verify the facts a bit before you involve and worry her about something that turns out to be totally irrelevant. Your fears might also be about her, of course. Childless mates won't be a lot of use, so the only real hope lies in other fathers-to-be.

The question is, how do you get access to them? Some may attend antenatal classes (more of which later) but these are often taken late on in the pregnancy. There are a few message boards online for dads only, but a glance through some of the more popular boards suggests that they are frequently invaded by mums-to-be, so they aren't generally too open and frank.

The truth – and the reason for this book's existence – is that true empathy is hard to find. I was lucky enough to have a couple of mates going through the process around the same time as me, but even then I didn't share experiences with them as often as I could, and should, have done. The fact is that you will get through by relying on a variety of different sources – an informative web site, a good book, a decent friend, an understanding partner. They can all help, but not one of them can give you all the answers.

Of course, Lindsay came home and reported that she'd gone 12 rounds with the little thug during a vital business meeting and I breathed a sigh of relief. I really, really should get out more.

• • •

Now I am getting out more. In a week Lindsay is going to pass over the baton to me as she begins her maternity leave and I start tutoring at a summer school in a local university. It's only seven weeks, but it gives me the chance to get a bit of perspective and get out from under the shadow of the scary heap of baby clothes catalogues that has appeared next to the sofa. I'm glad to be doing it. I love Lindsay dearly, but our conversation rarely deviates from the baby. This is made worse by the fact that this phase of pregnancy is regarded by most of the blokes I know as the dull bit – the long slide into the frenetic home straight.

Playing catch-up
Occupying yourself in the home straight

Do you remember that schooldays feeling of having holiday homework which you left untouched for weeks, only to find that you had to do it all in one panicked Sunday afternoon? That's the same feeling you'll get if, like me, you regard this time as 'the dull bit'. With me at work and Lindsay stuck at home, hot and virtually immobile, it was very hard to manage the large number of things we still hadn't done. We had to buy a car seat, a pram and a million other accessories in a blind panic before time disappeared from us completely. It might sound unbearably dull, but now is also the time to get cracking on all those major DIY jobs that need doing after the baby's born. For the first three months of the kid's life you'll have no time to even consider tackling such things, so get them in now while the world is moving at a gentle pace.

It'll also be good to get back into traditional roles for a while, especially if we decide to stay in them after the baby's born. I sometimes wonder whether after a couple of years of working from home I've become a weird hermit like freak of nature who can't communicate with his fellow men. At least I'll be at home in higher education.

Chapter Five
Ready or Not

Every summer of my childhood, I was treated to a trip to Dreamland amusement park in Margate. There was nothing particularly dreamlike about the place, though you could believe it had been asleep for about 100 years. The rides weren't exactly white-knuckle, more white haired.

My favourite was the Scenic Railway, a sort of flat roller coaster that spanned the perimeter of the park. It was slow and steady, but sometimes the cart would threaten to jump the warped and buckled tracks and there was an occasional slight incline that took an age to climb as the carts were ratcheted up a notch only to slide feebly down the other side.

I've thought about that ride throughout this pregnancy. There's no doubt I've felt that I'm on a fixed conveyor, that there's no going back or straying from the path. It's also true there's been the odd lump and bump along the way. Generally, though, it's been steady all the way. But now, hitting 30 weeks is like starting the painfully slow ascent before the shit scary drop into the oblivion of labour and birth. How do I take this plunge without losing my lunch?

Pedants may argue that it is the woman who faces the greater burden at this stage, but I say bullshit to that. My role is to stand on the sidelines and not interfere, not panic and not fall backwards over expensive monitoring equipment. It's not easy, and I need briefing on how to keep myself calm, cool and upright.

Ante-natal classes start next week, and I've got a free afternoon, so I'm going to go along to the first session. In my head I have a picture of a room full of women sitting on floor cushions panting and trying not to piss themselves, but I'm sure the reality is less appetising.

I need these classes badly. Over the last couple of weeks Lindsay has expanded her pregnancy vocabulary considerably, courtesy of the Pregnancy Channel or some such cable crap. She's also read every book available while pinned to the sofa by heat and fatigue. She keeps firing questions at me about different pain relief methods and birthing positions. I hadn't expected to be involved in this part of the decision making process, after all she's the one going through the pain, so I've guessed it's been up to her. If she wants drugs, give her drugs, I say. I'd want drugs. So far I've bluffed my way through it but I badly need a different response from "which do you think is best?" quickly followed by, "yes, that's what I was going to go for".

A lack of education on the subject can be dangerous in other ways. I'm reminded of the story about the American woman who overheard a medical term during labour that she thought was so beautiful, she picked it as a name for her daughter. You've no chance in life when you are called Meconium[1].

I don't want to put in the hours of research and bad television Lindsay has endured, yet if I'm going to be expected to participate in decision making I don't want to appear as thick as pig shit. What I need is clear, non-patronising, simple and effective preparation

---

[1] *It means newborn baby shit – I looked it up.*

for the rigours of the delivery suite. And where better to find it than at NHS antenatal classes?

•   •   •

I am never, ever going to another antenatal class in my life. OK, so that's mainly because I don't have any more free afternoons, but I'd also have to say that the experience wasn't entirely rewarding.

For starters it was just about the hottest day of the year so far, and the class was held in one of those rooms built in the 1970s as a large scale model of a microwave oven. We sat and dripped sweat from every orifice as the presiding health care woman – I never actually heard her job title – told us that there wouldn't be a midwife present due to ill health.

This woman was there to talk us through breathing techniques, pain relief and other key subjects. I mentally rubbed my hands – actually rubbing them together would have led to a sticky, sweaty mess – this was exactly the stuff I'd wanted to hear.

Unfortunately, I was the only partner who did want to hear it. As the sole representative in the room of a species that all the other hot, angry participants were slowly beginning to resent, I felt pretty uncomfortable.

Fortunately, the tension was eased by our hostess who singled me out while cracking such gems as "when the second stage of labour begins, you should really try not to be watching the football on TV, dad".

"I'll try," I replied feebly as the women around me snorted with ill concealed contempt. "Just as surely as I'll try not to fling my chair across the room at your fatuous, fat head," I added, in the car on the way home.

In between those comments I sat meekly and nodded appreciatively as required. I did the breathing exercise and I tried to absorb as much detail as I could. It was useful and constructive, but I got the feeling that I wasn't entirely welcome. That's odd, and what's even odder is the decision of our health authority to cancel the final, evening session of the antenatal classes which many working fathers could have attended. Again I'm met with the feeling that the professionals feel men are going to be no real use, so should be sidelined at all costs.

I'm pretty sure that's not a view shared by most mothers-to-be, so the only reason for it must simply be that it is tradition. But as our midwife said, in the course of her 30-something years in the job, the tradition has gone from regarding fathers in the delivery room as freaks to the complete opposite. Traditions change, that's the wonderful thing about evolution, that and the fact we no longer live in trees and eat bugs. So somewhere down the line, the man is going to have to be regarded by the system as a valued partner in pregnancy.

"A warm welcome to all you bastard son-of-a-bitch fathers-to-be"
Handling the antenatal class

I'm pleased to say that there are many health authorities a good deal more enlightened than ours, and these hold classes in the evenings or at times suitable to working fathers. If your health authority doesn't, it's probably because of a combination of staffing issues and a deep held belief that fathers-to-be wouldn't be fussed about going.

But good antenatal classes are an excellent preparation for your role in the delivery suite, and you shouldn't let the opportunity slide. So if you can't get time off, complain, and get others to do the same. If they won't change the timing, then the very least they should do is hold one dedicated session that deals with issues for fathers.

The antenatal class helped me feel a little less disorientated, but it hasn't lasted. A couple of days down the line and Lindsay has returned from another midwife check-up with a new and totally unexpected change of tack. She wants to have the baby at home.

Oh shit. As soon as she mentioned it, I realised two things – she is dead set on the idea, and I hate the idea more than anything in the world. This is a major problem.

My reservations are simple and, I think, justified. Our house, pleasant and comfortable though it is, has limited medical facilities. The midwives who have attended Lindsay to date in pregnancy are either unpredictable or extremely inexperienced. To trust the delivery of our baby to these kindly yet bumbling folks would be numbingly stupid. I can picture a huge range of nightmare scenarios in which we are faced with medical emergencies beyond our wildest fears and all I can do is boil water and serve up platefuls of biscuits as we wait for nature to sort out the mess. No, no and no. Over my dead body. End of story.

• • •

Not quite. Now that I come to think of it, a home birth might be quite a good idea, after all. OK, so I've still got a few minor reservations, but after reflection it's growing on me. Why the change of heart? I've spoken to a few parents in the last couple of days, and the responses have been amazingly similar. All the men have shaken their heads accompanied by the 'tut-tut-tut' beloved of repairmen. All the women have said that they wished they'd had home births. A surprising number actually did. They survived, their kids survived and maybe, just maybe it wasn't all by accident. Sixty years ago it was your only option, after all.

So I concluded that it is only men who have a real problem with home births. But why? Take our situation, we're just a few miles from the hospital, so if anything was to go wrong, we'd be seen as soon as possible. The positive effect of the relaxed home environment could be a real bonus in a long labour. I'd have all my home comforts and I could prepare meals and drinks. But the lingering doubts don't just go away, no matter how compelling the evidence. I claim that it's because I want to be sure that Lindsay and the baby are getting the best care throughout the process, but these fears are mine, they are about me and the level of guilt and responsibility I'd feel if something went wrong because I hadn't put my foot down. When do I accept that I should let go and just give Lindsay the support she needs to make the right decision for herself?

Later. I can take the chicken shit option of waiting, because if she goes into labour early, she goes into hospital, no question. If she goes past 37 weeks, we can have the debate then. Yeah, that'll work. You arsehole.

•   •   •

By an unspoken consensus, our sex life has come to an end until after the birth. We both have our reasons – Lindsay is suffering increasing discomfort in her hips and pelvis as the baby grows and I'm more than slightly spooked by the idea of being kicked by the baby in the throes of passion. I've always been a bit of a coy performer in the sexual arena, but bring in an audience and I'm totally shafted, so to speak.

Of course, but for Lindsay's physical and my emotional discomfort, we could be happily shagging away until the baby is due. It doesn't harm the baby and it does a lot to counteract the stress of the final few weeks. It is also one of the more believable old wives' remedies for bringing on an overdue labour.

Left hand down a bit
Sex in pregnancy (part two)

Sex at this stage in pregnancy is an art form, like a very complex and sweaty game of Twister. It is all about position and communication – while you won't hurt the baby, you'll probably end up hurting yourself or your partner if things aren't well planned in advance. We aren't talking Kama Sutra here, just a slight deviation from the old-fashioned missionary position. Trust me when I say that forcing her to lie uncomfortably on her back for hours while you steam away above her is not pleasurable. It might just about qualify as preparation for the long and tiresome period of lying prone in the delivery room, but that wouldn't do you any justice as a lover. You are pretty safe with her on top, because she can keep control – though having your belly slapped by a huge bulge is a tad weird. Best bet is either the side-on 'spoon' position (good sensation, crap penetration) or all fours (which can get quite tiring for her).

When we stopped having sex for a while earlier in the pregnancy, it was largely my fault. Lack of communication and education was to blame. I was worried that I'd harm the baby, or that I'd hurt Lindsay. If I'd talked to her more frankly it might have resolved things quicker. But this time, though we rarely speak openly about the subject, there's been plenty of communication. She is suffering – tired, sore and a bit irritable. She lets me know, via gentle nudges and firm kicks, that I should be getting back into hired slave mode. Not being around all the time makes that hard, but when I am home, I try to be supportive.

A lot of what she's going through is beyond my puny help. The worst thing is the tiredness, I'd guess. Not only does she find lying down uncomfortable, she has to get up repeatedly in the night to pee. Sometimes I wonder whether nature is just a great big hidden camera stunt, designed to make humanity look really dumb. It certainly seems unreasonably cruel at times.

"Are you awake?"
Her changing sleep pattern

A couple of months later, when the experience had the rosy glow of hindsight, Lindsay described a typical night to me. She'd get into bed, shift herself onto her side, tuck a pillow between her legs and drop off straight away. An hour or so later she'd wake, stiff as a board and desperate to change position. She'd have to sit up, remove the pillow, move herself painfully onto her other side, then set it all up again, only to discover that she needed to have a piss.

It was a miracle that I stayed asleep with all that going on next to me. It's a hard time for your partner, her womb is doing its best to flatten her bladder, so it fills in no time, and this, the aches and pain, kicks and movements are keeping her awake. What can you do about it? Not a lot – if she's at home and filling her day with chores you could take on a few more, freeing her up for a guilt free afternoon nap. You could buy her a shaped pillow (available from specialist baby and mother care shops) that supports her body.

Your main objective is to remove all the minor stresses – bills, families, shopping, cleaning, washing – that she can't deal with while she's putting up with all the crap nature is hitting her with. Relaxation and breathing techniques work for some women, and as she's well past the six months stage of pregnancy, you could buy her some aromatherapy oils or salts for a chill out late night bath. Check with the shop that the ones you're getting are suitable for pregnancy.

We keep getting messages from friends and family saying that we should be getting all the sleep we can at this stage 'because we're really going to need it after'. Thanks, guys. Big help.

Dream on
Your changing sleep pattern

Actually, it is good advice. I wish I'd taken it. If she can't sleep, you won't help her by staying awake in sympathy. As one of the surveyed fathers explained, sleep is going to be at a premium from onset of labour until God knows when. You need yours now.

Now that the summer school has finished, I'm back home full time. It's just as well, Lindsay's mobility has been on a steady decline over the last few weeks, and now she can't drive or walk the dogs. I am needed more than ever and I think that is probably an annoyance for her. For me, it's a taste of what's to come, a hint of future responsibilities.

I've been thinking a lot about fatherhood. It still feels like quite an abstract idea, but I find myself wondering again what sort of a father I'll be. My own dad has always been quietly caring without being excessively emotional. He has always stepped back when I want to be free and stepped forwards when I want help. I could do a lot worse.

And yet I want to be a bit different. For starters I want to be more hands-on than my dad was. I want to share the burden of care a bit more equally, though of course I haven't the faintest idea about the reality of looking after a baby. I might hate the idea when it comes to it. But I want to try. If I screw up then I can try my hand at something else, like gardening or collecting vintage toy cars.

Maybe I just shouldn't think about it at all. If, as all and sundry never tire of telling me, I am going to be taken completely by surprise, then I should just sit back and let it happen. A good friend of mine set about fatherhood with all the ill advised good intentions of a DIY enthusiast trying to construct a Swedish wardrobe. He found himself totally confused by the resulting balls-up. There are no instructions, no map, no straightforward answers, just experience and trial and error.

• • •

It looks like my cowardly decision to put off the home birth debate has worked, though to be honest, I wish it hadn't. The reason a home birth is ruled out is that Lindsay's painful hip is worse than ever. She's been given crutches by the hospital physiotherapist and is really struggling to get around. It's a thoroughly miserable situation, rendered all the more crap by the fact that we can't go anywhere or do anything that takes her mind off her discomfort.

"That's new, isn't it?"
Dealing with her changing body

Lindsay's mobility problems were really bad, and fortunately for most women things don't get that extreme. But symptoms do get a bit scary for both of you at this late stage. Your partner's body is changing in long and short term ways – immediate issues might include swollen ankles, her skin might be feeling uncomfortable and itchy, she'll be exhausted and sometimes miserable. Generally, these symptoms can be eased by resting – which means more chores for you right now. Longer term change might mean varicose veins and stretch marks. You might find these ugly. Chances are you won't find them attractive, but then nor will she.

Your role here is all about sensitivity and tact. While varicose veins can be eased with exercise, that doesn't make a happy combination with swollen ankles. As for stretch marks, well just don't go there. Not all women get them, but if your partner does, remember that she's got something the size and weight of a bowling ball inside her, and her body can't hope to take the strain without some blemish. If you want to push her into getting back to that perfect pre-pregnancy figure, maybe you should try getting back to the weight and fitness level of your 18 year old self first. No? Thought not.

We're in some kind of bizarre Groundhog Day situation at the hospital, we keep going to see the consultant, who is never there, and his registrars keep telling us that everything's fine and Lindsay should be OK for a natural birth. The only trouble is that while they all agree on this point, one of them thinks an epidural painkiller would be a good idea, while another thinks it would cause more damage. The physiotherapist doesn't want to intervene and no one wants to commit. And absolutely no one seems to have any suggestions for dealing with the pain now.

I hate the hospital. I didn't like the sight of it on that first traumatic visit a lifetime ago for the emergency scan and I still despise it. What I hate most of all is the fact that my wife is forced to sit for hours on end, only to repeat her story to every new face she sees. By now, there are tears of frustration in her eyes each time we visit and nothing is done. All we see is a stream of people who have excellent explanations for why it isn't their fault or their responsibility. When we started seeing the consultants, I felt a bit odd watching them manipulate Lindsay's belly and abdomen, especially the men. As a partner you're not normally party to these essential but very personal interactions with someone else. I wouldn't go so far as to say I've been feeling jealous, but I have started to get more protective, especially as the examinations have become more painful.

As Lindsay has got more stressed and frustrated by the endless parade of doctors, I've been able to employ a successful tactic from my dealings with the midwife. We talk things through before each appointment and I generally make a list of all the questions we want answered. Lindsay is rarely in the right state of mind to remember everything, so I provide a pretty good back-up.

Attacks, cracks and quacks
Medical problems and the hospital

Late in the game, we discovered the possibility that Lindsay's problem might have been a form of SPD – not the German political party, but a disorder affecting the pubic bone in pregnancy. It limits mobility and can cause real pain prior to labour. For some people, it can even lead to lasting damage. Unfortunately, the medical profession is yet to make up its collective mind whether the condition exists at all. Believe me, guys, it does.

We encountered midwives who knew about the disorder and were sympathetic, and we met other, normally more senior, staff who basically believed that it was all in the mind. If your partner is getting a lot of pain or discomfort in the pubic area around now, there's a support group for the disorder and plenty of information on the internet (try **www.nctpregnancyandbaby care.com** or call the NCT on 0870 770 3236). Don't be fobbed off and don't make the mistake of always believing something just because a doctor tells you it. Remember – 'trust her instincts'.

Even the officious hospital receptionists are starting to recognise Lindsay by her distinctive limp and agonised expression. We've started to get something close to human sympathy from them. Secretly I think this has less to do with Lindsay's plight and more to do with the fact that admin people always love to get one over on their professional colleagues. They tut sadly as we explain how hard it is to get anyone to take us seriously, then promise to do all they can to fight on our behalf – perhaps by ordering the wrong sort of paper clips or something.

One thing they have done is to ensure that we can been seen by the actual consultant at our next appointment. Though whether he'll make any difference remains to be proved.

• • •

He's made a difference. He listened and seemed to know how to respond, how to put our minds at ease, but more than anything else he made a difference by deciding that Lindsay's wait has been long and painful enough. He booked her in for induction of labour next week. Next week? Oh shit.

She'll be at full term according to our dates, but it's still one hell of a shock to the system to know that she's now a ticking time bomb. The moment she goes into the delivery suite, she is staying there until the baby is born. In other words, I'm going to be a father in a matter of days.

Cue panic. I am the least prepared father-to-be in the whole world. There must be a bag to pack. No, there's two bags to pack, one for Lindsay, one for the baby. But what to put in? So far my mental list consists of the following – toy for the baby, hat for the baby bought from football club shop (size six months plus), copy of the Radio Times and chocolate bars. To my surprise none of these items is on the official list which Lindsay patiently handed me. Except for the hat, but not this hat, I could use this hat as a carry cot.

Calm down. Everything is in hand, mysteriously purchased by the shopping fairies. We've got little bodysuits and sleep suits and non-gender specific clothes and socks, boots, mittens, sheets, towels. The baby's bag is bigger than Lindsay's – a taste of what's to come, I fear. Lindsay's bag is filled with clothes that look like something from a Victorian Ann Summers party, heavy black dresses with holes in the chest where she can stick the baby's head without causing distress in public by forcing men to stare at her breasts. These weird clothes are about as interesting as the pre-birth maternity gear she's had to wear, most of which is shapeless and dark, none of which is any good in the summer. At least she's never had to wear dungarees.

We've offloaded the dogs onto Lindsay's parents, who are, understandably, nervous and excited about the big event. We made this decision to give them something to do because it takes their minds off things, but it also keeps them tied safely to their home 100 miles away. After weeks of softening them up for the news, we've gently explained that we won't be expecting to see them at the hospital – in fact all relatives, friends and well-wishers are banned until we get home again. On the plus side that means I get quality time with Lindsay and the baby, on the minus side it means I'm on my own if things go wrong.

I don't want to think about that. I've packed the bags, checked and rechecked everything and even placed them hopefully at the bottom of the stairs. Now all I have to do is wait for a week until Lindsay goes in to hospital.

"So where's the pool table?"
Visiting the delivery suite

If your partner's going to have a hospital delivery, there's a good chance that the maternity wing will let the pair of you have a wander round the place to get familiar with the layout. These tours are normally conducted once a week in groups. They'll almost certainly be on a weekday, which means more time off work, but it's worthwhile. You'll be feeling pretty disorientated when you're there for real, so this dry run just gives you an idea of where the bogs are and whether there's a place to make a coffee or a snack.

Waiting with a goal in sight is easily preferable to life before the consultant. Until the decision to induce, Lindsay faced the prospect of another month of misery. All she has to cope with now is a few days of watching me race around like an idiot.

Pull yourself together man
Getting organised and buying a car seat

While I was faffing around with my headless chicken act, there was a range of useful things I could have been doing. It would have been good to get hold of a plan of the hospital – parking was always a nightmare, and I didn't have a clue where to take her in an emergency. Similarly, I hadn't made any contingency travel plans in case the direct route to the hospital was blocked. I didn't have the midwife's emergency number in my wallet, nor did I have the numbers of friends and family. They're all mundane things, but they need attention, and it'll make both you and your partner feel at ease if you've got them covered.

This is also the time to catch up on any outstanding essential shopping, including enough food for you and your partner for a week or so after she comes out of hospital. You can just about get away without buying a single thing for the baby up to this point, except for a few outfits, nappies and somewhere to sleep – but if you're going to bring the kid home from hospital by car you have to have a car seat.

There are two types of seat available from birth, one for babies up to 10kg (around nine months) and one for babies up to 13kg (around 15 months). The first of these generally gives better support for smaller babies, though if your baby is really small, you'll probably need extra padding in the seat to keep it secure. You can swap to a bigger, forward facing seat at the 13kg milestone. Until your baby reaches that weight, you should put the seat so that it faces the rear of the car, and never put it on a front seat with an airbag.

Other good tips are to get the seat fitted by a decent store and learn how to fit it properly yourself – incorrect fitting seriously affects performance. Try before you buy as not all seats fit all cars. And don't be tempted to buy a seat second hand. If it's been damaged or in an accident it will be dangerous.

Of course, she'd really like it to be over now, and I have to balance my desire to put it off until I'm a grown-up with the wish to see the baby and end Lindsay's suffering. The midwife at the hospital said we should try a few old tricks to bring the baby on. Her first two suggestions were long walks and lots of sex, which almost got her a clump round the head with a crutch, but then she quickly added the other recommendations of hot curries and raspberry leaf tea. Not one of these remedies constitutes official medical opinion, but they do make good common sense. Walking and sex keep you healthy and lithe, a hot curry is a shock to the system and raspberry tea is so horrible you want to give birth just to avoid drinking another drop. But then, as Lindsay pointed out after my third cup, she's the one who is supposed to drink the tea.

In all honesty I'm hoping that none of these remedies work. I can deal with taking Lindsay into the hospital on a nice pre-planned, leisurely afternoon drive. But I don't fancy the thought of a bleary eyed midnight scramble, or a desperate call dragging me back from a meeting. We've had to turn down party invitations because they are too far from the hospital, and I've even cut back on the booze in the evenings, just in case I'm expected to drop everything at a moment's notice.

● ● ●

Another side-effect of spotting life at the end of the tunnel is that we've started to think about the baby again. For a couple of months Lindsay's well-being has dominated our thoughts. The baby has taken care of itself, as we have been repeatedly assured it would.

But all that time, except for a few wistful thoughts, we hadn't really focused on the person inside my wife's belly, the little stranger sapping her strength, who is finally going to make an appearance.

Most of the talk had been about gender, which hasn't really been a hot topic since the anatomy scan. I remain undecided, and I'd be willing to trust Lindsay's instinct on the subject, except she still doesn't seem to have one. In my heart I know that I'd cope better with a boy than a girl. I'm destined to be overprotective in either case, but a boy might just stand half a chance of being independent. But having been a little boy myself, I can't help thinking what foul beasts they can be. Perhaps a girl would be better.

We're not really doing any better with names, though we've tried all sorts of scientific methods. We made a tentative start months ago with a baby names book, scanning through page after page of names, calling out favourites. This quickly degenerated into calling out the stupidest names we could find and pretty soon we gave up altogether. Now, though, I've got the book out again with serious intent and I've devised a system where we go through it, writing down our top five in secret, then comparing answers to find the best placed preferable option. Simple. Except our top fives featured totally different names. So it's back to square one. Some families pass on names like heirlooms, we don't have that simplicity of choice as I can't think of anyone in either of our immediate families who would actually want us to recycle their name. No, it's got to be our choice.

In this, as in most things, Lindsay has been the one who's developed the more philosophical attitude. She says there's no point in finding and agreeing a name that might not fit the baby. So we'll hang on until we're properly introduced.

•   •   •

There's a couple of major, pressing issues that I just can't bring myself to discuss with Lindsay. The first, and worse, is something that has emerged from the endless cable show births that are ever present on our TV. It's something that keeps me awake all night. I

absolutely, definitely, unquestionably don't want to cut the umbilical cord. This is a new tradition, and I'm sure a load of fathers have
managed it and felt that it made them a real part of the delivery.
But I really don't want to do it. It isn't out of fear, but out of concern – I can't cut my own fingernails without slicing open an artery.
If I'm coerced into performing anything medical, it'll be fatal for all
concerned.

To be fair, I don't think it will take much to convince Lindsay of
the logic of this decision. She's seen my attempts at DIY.

The other big fear is change. I'm not talking about my future, here,
just my coinage. With a week to go before the big day, and with
those bags packed, my sole remaining useful function is to amass
and hoard enough coins to pay for the hospital parking. I've turned
into Rain Man. I keep counting the coins and putting them away,
getting them out again, counting them again. It's hypnotic. And it
helps to distract me from the fact that I am shit scared and underprepared.

•　　•　　•

As if Lindsay hasn't had enough misery, her induction has now
been delayed three times. We've been sat at home, packed and
ready to go for days now. We don't really talk, such is the atmos-
phere of stress and frustration. All we do is sit, tense and alert,
watching trash on TV and trying not to get each other worked up.
It is the most horrible wait, though I have my precious coins for
company. The hospital keep insisting that we call in every few
hours to see if there's a spare bed. It is agony.

•　　•　　•

The miracle finally happens. There's a bed. We're going in.

Chapter Six
Twist and Shout

In stark contrast to conception, labour is a slow process. We've spent the best part of five hours this evening sitting around in the God forsaken delivery suite, with Lindsay hitched up to a machine that measures exactly how far she is from the end of what is gradually becoming a living hell.

This interminable wait is a chronic pain in the arse, especially as it has come hard on the heels of the equally long, equally frustrating wait to be allowed into the damned place. I've read every single celebrity magazine published in the last six months and am now an aficionado of Jade's bowel movements (loose, frequent) and Jordan's implants (frequently loose). Lindsay is exhausted, depressed and disillusioned. I'm just hungry and hot.

Why are hospitals so excessively heated? All the books tell us that a baby shouldn't be overheated, and God knows the poor, flushed pregnant women don't need any more warming up. Perhaps it is some kind of puritanical desire to make fathers-to-be sweat, just so they'll think twice about ever shagging again, so they don't come back and use up more National Health resources. I've never been so uncomfortable and I'm not the one being poked and prodded by a bizarre assortment of midwives.

"Now, where did I put my trouser press?"
Your hospital survival kit

Like Lindsay, your partner will almost certainly get a long list of items to bring to hospital. These rarely include any seriously practical items for the men. Depending on your situation, you might be in the delivery suite or on the ward for a couple of days. Most men will be stuck in the place for a good 12 hour stretch before, during and after delivery.

So you'll need some proper food and drink – hospital facilities are generally pretty grim (think school meals without the nutritional value) and the shops and cafes generally open during regular hours only. You'll need to remember the camera, which won't be high on your partner's priority list. You'll also need lots of things to read and maybe a walkman – though it is nice to believe that you'll spend all your time whispering encouragement to your partner, that can become dull after the first day or so.

You also need to dress like a mountaineer, plenty of layers – the heat of wards and delivery suites can be overwhelming, but you'll probably be glad of the chance to get some air at some stage, especially if it's an all nighter. Take a phone by all means, but don't expect to use it anywhere but outside. If it's pissing down, your loved ones probably won't appreciate a quick text message. So take some change for the payphones.

One thing I've noticed in these lengthy hours of being bored shitless is that hospital midwives are either huge or tiny. There seems to be no middle ground – perhaps they all start off large and sweat themselves down to withered, frail, dehydrated souls. I sincerely hope so.

The strangest part of this waiting game is the knowledge that it will end suddenly and dramatically. I'm worried about the pain Lindsay faces and I'm worried about the effort I'm going to have to put in to help her cope. I can suddenly see the great advantage in nipping off to the pub for a few hours and then coming back once the job's done. The prospect of copious alcohol is tempting right now, but not as tempting as the prospect of shirking all my responsibility and letting someone else deal with the forthcoming mess.

Up on the ward, I'm worried about something other than the long wait or the high temperatures. Lindsay is, like most people, fairly private – especially at a time like this when she doesn't exactly feel like socialising. There's no alternative on this ward, however, a huge corridor of women moaning, groaning, snoring, crying and generally keeping each other awake. Lindsay's new temporary home is on an end section with one new mum and another mum-to-be. It's a forbidding place, and, of course, it's hot as hell. As soon as she's settled I make my excuses and leave.

• • •

Back at home things are even worse. With the dogs at Lindsay's parents it's just me and the self-obsessed cats. One of them complained bitterly at me as I came into the dark, cold house. I narrowly avoided stepping on a mouse she'd caught in the kitchen, while I scrambled around looking for some food. I settled on some crisps, chocolate, cold cuts and red wine. It's important to keep my strength up.

I have the place to myself. While this may normally be an opportunity to watch sport in the nude or try to make out the breasts on the scrambled adult channels while chain drinking bottles of beer, I feel shattered. Instead of the above I had a long, hot bath and lay staring lazily at my apologetic, shrunken genitals. They are to blame, and they know it. I woke up with a start and sent a great splat of water over the bathroom floor, soaking the cat and making her run around with gratifying animation.

Tomorrow is, more likely than not, the day on which my wife will give birth to our first child. The thought is so petrifying that I just can't allow myself to dwell on it. Every time I let my mind wander over what lies ahead, I come back to the endless births we have watched on those shitty cable shows. Half of them are agonising natural deliveries in rough British inner cities, with knuckleduster encrusted mothers swearing and sweating while their hideous, toothless husbands suck nervously on a roll-up in the waiting area. The other half are beautiful, overpopulated American delivery suite births where the baby slips out effortlessly and everyone hugs while the Pregnancy Planner gushes the words "good job" at the rosy cheeked, serene mother. Somehow, I didn't picture either scenario. In fact, I simply don't know what to expect at all. Whatever happened to being cool and prepared? This is like one of those dreams where you turn over the exam paper only to find the questions are all in Japanese. But I really can't afford to fail the test tomorrow.

$$\bullet \quad \bullet \quad \bullet$$

Slept about four hours last night. Feel like shit. Feel much better than Lindsay, who had the typical night of unnecessary disturbance that only a hospital can provide.

She was sitting up, picking over some breakfast when I arrived. After about an hour of riveting conversation on the subject of my every waking movement away from her, I ran out of things to say. Sure, we could talk about the need to redecorate the bedroom, or possible defensive formations in the forthcoming England match, but this would be redundant small talk. The big issue is the baby, but neither of us feels like talking about it. The fact remains that we've potentially got 13 hours together to sit and dwell on where the hell this kid has got to.

A few hours later and there's not a lot to report. Lindsay has been for another examination and a further dose of the induction gel that's supposed to get things cracking. I've invented excuses to wander the halls of the hospital, pounding my way around the echoing corridors while gazing with barely concealed horror at the sheer range of things that can go wrong with the human body. A door smashed open with undue noise as a trolley appeared with its obligatory grey faced zombie – pushing another patient to theatre no doubt.

Scarier still was the scene that greeted me in the main concourse of the hospital. The place has been decked out in fancy decorations and strewn with ghastly teddy bears in anticipation of the arrival of a couple of reality TV 'stars' who are coming to perform some celebrity CPR on the hospital's bank balance.

I confess I was warned of this horror. Earlier this morning, the girl in the bed opposite Lindsay was babbling about some kind of cake sale the midwives were organising, as if they had time to spare from drinking coffee and smoking in the store cupboard. This girl is a reliable source, she appears to be a 'lifer', able to give a short critique of each member of the nursing staff – 'she's alright', 'watch her, she's a right bitch' etc – as well as full biographical and biological details of the other inmates... sorry, patients. I get the impression that if I bring her some smokes she might even be able to get Lindsay's labour speeded up. It may yet come to that.

So while I was stood in the foyer, watching hundreds of medical professionals distract themselves from their life saving jobs, I started to get even more nervous about what's to come. What if the person who's supposed to care for my wife and child is too busy fawning over some talentless prick out here?

Patently unable to wrap my wife in cotton wool, I opted for the next best thing and bought her a big bag of it from the pharmacy, and then got a pile of magazines and papers from the shop. When all else fails, read – it might take our minds off the prospect that our baby could well be delivered live on telly by Charlie Dimmock.

"Fine, I'll just have to deliver it myself"
Remaining patient and positive

I can't predict your experience of labour, and I wouldn't try – but one thing I'm pretty sure you will experience is that gnawing feeling of powerlessness that was starting to overwhelm me as I waited around for something to happen. Whether it comes in the delivery suite itself or earlier there is a good chance that you'll find yourself anxious to get things moving, but unable to do a thing about it.

You need to accept that this is not what you are about at this stage – responsibility for that part of your partner's welfare has been passed over to the hospital staff. But you can maintain some control by ensuring that your partner's wishes for the birth are met. If she's made a birth plan – a list of practical dos and don'ts like whether to have pain killing drugs in labour or a jab to help deliver the placenta – make certain you have a copy and that you know what it all means.

We wrote a plan that detailed Lindsay's pelvic and hip problems, made multiple copies of it and stuffed it into every face we encountered. The woman who ran the antenatal class described how women elevate to a higher plane in the final stage of labour, which is all very well for them, but it rather takes their eye off what the medics are up to. You will need to keep an eye out to make sure that, where medically possible, her wishes are being respected.

Lunch has come and gone and been followed by another examination and dose of gel. This left Lindsay reeling, like a kick from a mule, and the exam was really painful. Not for the first time, I felt a strong desire to thump the midwife who was causing my wife such unnecessary pain – especially as this one was wearing a teddy badge and a soppy grin which suggested that her mind was far away – probably in the back of a celebrity's limo trying to prove the adage about nurses being a sure thing.

Something that isn't so sure is whether our baby's going to arrive today. After a lot of pain and prodding, Lindsay's back on the ward and none the wiser. The midwives keep attaching her to a machine that measures contractions and the baby's heart, then they come along at 20 minute intervals, take a look at the printout, nod their heads and say "another 20 minutes" as if she's a beef joint. I've finished my newspaper and I'm back onto the celebrity magazines. I wonder if it's too late to get down to the foyer for an autograph.

·   ·   ·

Drama, pure and simple. Firstly, the woman in the next bed, who has complained of headaches for a few days, is rushed off to have emergency brain surgery, then Lindsay starts having some serious contractions.

Her poor neighbour's dilemma has left Lindsay without a midwife – the only one on duty having disappeared with her patient in a helicopter. Quite why a midwife is a useful appendage during emergency brain surgery I'm not quite clear. Anyhow, the seriousness of the situation has kept us from complaining unnecessarily about Lindsay's plight.

Sadly, a couple of hours after contractions started in earnest, complaints aren't unnecessary any more. There's still no staff on the ward and Lindsay is suffering. I always thought there would be something vaguely entertaining about contractions. I pictured Lindsay with a look of intense concentration on her face, puffing and blowing like a miniature train, while I rubbed her back, held her hand and withstood a volley of abuse that would make a navvy blush. But in reality they were almost as painful to watch as they were to endure, she squeezed my hand and winced and seemed to slip away from me to a higher plane of agony each time one struck, as they did with increasing regularity, recording sharply on the monitor like mounting tremors.

We rang the emergency buzzer and someone came to tell us that the staff were changing over and wouldn't be available for about an hour. Changing over? An hour? These people aren't manning a nuclear submarine, for Christ's sake, they are attending to the incredibly similar needs of a ward of women. And yet, despite the fact that this patently isn't rocket science, they do seem to take a scientific approach to having a coffee and a gossip. If only I had a rocket.

Meanwhile, Lindsay's suffering is increasing and I've had enough. I know I'm not the only person in the world whose partner has suffered in labour, but to be frank, I don't give a shit about anyone else. It's time for someone to act.

"Do you know who I am?"
Complaining and coping in an emergency

So what happens when things really do go wrong? If your partner is in pain it isn't easy meekly waiting your turn to be seen. But it's equally hard for the midwives to have their agenda set by whichever father-to-be shouts the loudest. You have to step back and trust the judgement of the professionals. They might be overworked, they might be tired and unsympathetic, but they are the experts. If you're really uncomfortable with the treatment your partner is getting then complain, but be firm, insistent and polite. Don't shout, and don't threaten to sue, mainly because you'll feel like a total prick afterwards.

Salvation comes in many forms, and ours has come in the shape of a small, feisty midwife from the North East. After finally emerging from her mammoth handover she took one look at Lindsay's chart and declared her ready to go down to the delivery suite. She then proceeded to attempt another examination and that's when the problems started.

Lindsay's hip mobility has declined so much since the first use of the induction gel and now she can barely move her legs without yelping with pain. The contractions were like a picnic compared to this experience. The midwife seemed to get frustrated with her, then remembered herself and grew more sympathetic when she saw that Lindsay was desperately unhappy.

By this stage I was totally redundant, I had tears of frustration in my eyes and I could barely look at the pain etched on her face. I had to do something, though, and meekly suggested that I didn't see how Lindsay was going to be able to squeeze this baby out of legs clamped tighter than a nun's at an orgy. The midwife agreed, more or less, and finally said out loud what we'd been thinking for a while – Lindsay was going to need a Caesarean.

Another slice of life
Surgery and Caesarian sections

Despite a lot of crap in the media about the 'too posh to push' generation, most women I know would much rather have a natural labour. It isn't hard to see why – a major operation, a great big scar and no driving or lifting for six weeks as opposed to a few – albeit agonising – hours of pushing, puffing and panting. Most men I know would rather see their partners undergo something 'natural' instead of being cut open.

Caesarean sections are 'bad' because they are expensive for hospitals, but in many cases they are a vital emergency option. A true emergency C-section would normally be done because of a complication in labour, and would be carried out under general anaesthetic, which is scary in itself, and is made worse by the fact that the man is not allowed into the operating the-atre. An elective C-section, where there is no pressing medical danger, is normally done under local anaesthetic and you can be present throughout.

Now there's another agonising wait while the powers that be fart about trying to decide whether Lindsay should actually be allowed the operation that she so patently needs. But what she also needs is a painkiller, as the contractions are still coming hard and fast. She can't have anything until they've made a decision on the C-section.

To mitigate the pain, the staff have at least allowed Lindsay to hob-ble down to the delivery suite. Every movement seems to be ago-nising, from the closing of the lift door to the jolt as it finishes its descent. I'm done with being meek now, I'm not going to tolerate any other course of action, even though I have absolutely no idea whether this is the best thing for her.

My concern is, in part, selfish. I don't want to see any more of this pain. I know now that I would have struggled desperately with the idea of a natural labour. It is humbling and embarrassing to note how easily I've crumbled into a desire to fix everything quickly. But as far as I can see, nothing means more than the here and now and I'm scared, for her, for me, for the baby.

• • •

Everything else is a blur. Well, that's not strictly true, it's all etched on my memory, but it was so bizarre and dreamlike I can only tell it in a slightly awed retrospect, as if explaining the plot of some fan-tastic film I've just seen.

The story, in a nutshell, is this: couple arrive at delivery suite, close to tears and state of collapse, yet ready for a fight. Feisty and scary Geordie midwife leans on meek delivery suite midwife until Caesarean becomes only option, midwife consults senior doctor on duty who agrees to operation. Forms are filled in, serious talk is given and husband is sent out to get baby's gear from boot of car. All in the space of about half an hour.

As far as I could make out, the male lead in this drama was played by this bloke who had a split personality. On the one hand, he thought that he was some sort of medical expert – he got himself dressed up in a blue suit with a weird shower cap and rinsed his hands, shaking the water droplets off in the time honoured senior surgeon style. On the other hand, the same bloke was reduced to a grinning, grimacing wreck, forced to sit in humiliated silence on a garden chair in the corner of a room while his wife was prepared for an operation.

Like all movies, the reality of this was a lot duller than the artifice – Lindsay's bed was wheeled into a room that looked like some kind of workshop, I guessed it was a side room that they used as a holding bay for pre-op women. A paint spattered beat box was playing some tinny Robbie Williams songs in the background. I half expected the caretaker to come in and start washing his brushes in the sink.

They got poor Lindsay sitting up and moaned that she couldn't get her legs high enough for the injection into her spine. Everyone, even the battling anaesthetist, seemed too relaxed. I wasn't relaxed and I was wearing a blue suit, the type that surgeons wear.

Then the senior doctor who had given the go-ahead for the operation came in, dressed in gear almost as important looking as mine, and starting getting ready to operate. This was the stage where I could have stopped him, demanded to see his credentials, certificates etc. I could have got him to try a practice cut somewhere discreet, so that I could check out how steady his hand was. Was that alcohol I smelt on his breath? No, it was being spread all over

Lindsay's back, a weird kind of cherry brandy like substance. But not, I guessed – by now familiar with the medical world – actually cherry brandy.

The spinal block was proving troublesome, and another anaesthetist was paged, just like in real life medical TV drama shows. I began to fear that the staff had exceeded their capabilities. But right at the last minute the anaesthetist managed to get the needle in, what a genius. All was ready.

A small windbreak was set up to protect Lindsay from the sight of her soon to be open belly, and I was allowed to shuffle my plastic chair over to be with her. She was shivering uncontrollably and suddenly I thought something dreadful must be wrong. I looked around at all the medical people getting on with their jobs and whimpered something about Lindsay's shaking. Don't worry, it's normal they all replied, automatically, each one of them thinking 'get this tosser out of the theatre'. For though it resembled a tatty broom cupboard, a theatre it well and truly was. And just to hammer the point home, the surgeon started to cut.

I quickly developed a nasty case of tennis fan's neck, switching my rapt attention between Lindsay's bewildered face and the surgeon's intense concentration. Was that a twinge of pain? No, 15 love. Was that a look of concern? No, 15 all. He called for forceps. Is that good? Yes, I think so, 15 – 30. He disappeared and grunted with unconcealed effort. Was he struggling to free the baby? It didn't seem so, 15 – 40.

A thin, plaintive, slightly pathetic cry and the game was over. The surgeon had won, and was holding a trophy high in the air, a deep pink trophy with a purple umbilical cord twisting like a phone flex.

His assistant beamed down at us. "Do you want to know what it is?"

"No," I replied, "We want to wait until its 18th birthday. What do you think, you stupid bitch."

"Yes," I replied, meekly cowering next to my shivering wife.

"It's a boy," she said.

Of course it is. How could it possibly be anything else? Only a boy can become simultaneous captain of the England football and cricket teams. Only a tough, rough little male can be a virile, sexually active yet charming Romeo with a penis like a fire hose. The minute I saw him, this scrawny, crumpled rag of a boy, I knew he was going to be the first emperor of the known universe. And I knew that I'd always really known that, to tell the truth.

No guts, no glory
Coping with all that blood

All the blood and other strange fluid is common in almost all types of delivery, and it can be a bit scary, but now is not the time to scream 'what have you done?' and fling yourself protectively across your partner's body. The trick is to take your lead from the attitude and expressions of the midwives, or the doctors. They have a habit of being brusque and professional, but when things go wrong they'll get worried just like anyone. So whatever's happening around you, if they are calm, stay calm.

Back to that penis again. While they were getting Lindsay stitched up, the midwife took me and the boy through the disconcerting rivers of blood and gunk into the recovery room, where she dressed him while I stood gibbering by her side.

The assistant in this room glanced across at us and asked about the baby's sex. "It's a boy," the midwife said. "A well endowed boy."

"Takes after his father," I said, quick as a flash. What took a little longer was the slow realisation that this comment seemed to suggest I was either: A. hitting on an elderly midwife minutes after my wife had given birth; B. boasting about my genitalia in a juvenile and plainly exaggerated manner; or C. talking out of my arse.

As it turned out, my cock and bull story passed without comment from either woman, and I was able to sink gracelessly into another plastic chair, holding my son for the first time. God, he looked awful. He didn't look as bad as some of those freakish babies with conical heads, or ones with faces like gargoyles, but he did have a lot of blood and mess on him and though my paternal instinct was to kiss him tenderly, my gut reaction said he'd be much better off with a firm handshake.

"Hurry up love, we're missing the match"
How to handle a natural labour

Once the drama had died down, I found myself wondering what a natural delivery would have been like. Lindsay went through the contractions and a hell of a lot of pain, and most of the emotions I experienced were similar to those of a father involved in a natural delivery. But we didn't have to face the reality of hours in the delivery room, and that's probably something I'll never experience.

Statistics suggest that you are more likely to go through it than any other form of delivery, so, for the record here's some advice from one of the surveyed fathers: "You need to be mentally prepared for your partner's labour – it's probably best to do something like smash your kneecap and then lock yourself in a room with her for 12 hours".

The surveyed fathers – most of whom went through natural deliveries with their partners – ranged in their experiences from feeling like a spare part who just got in the way, to a key part of the process. Generally it seems that the more prepared, relaxed and focused on your partner's needs you are, the better the experience. You should also remember the two crucial standbys of praise and reassurance for your partner. But of all these, simply being there for her is the biggest, most effective thing you will do.

It was all over pretty quickly after that. They wheeled Lindsay in and took our picture, marvelling at the quality of our camera. By now I was taking every compliment as personal approval of my virility, so I just beamed with considerable pride and a little embarrassment for the sake of the lesser men in the room. Just before we went back up to the ward, I was made to go and take off my dressing-up clothes. In the prep room, there was another father-to-be getting ready. I swaggered up to him, laughing amiably, patted him on the shoulder and assured him everything would be just great. And to be fair, for his part, he looked at me as if I was a complete tosser.

Then it was back to the ward – a side ward without awful sick people thank God – a quick kiss goodnight for my family and, as the credits rolled, I was unceremoniously packed off home.

Driving through the dead streets at 1am, it felt like I was on a different planet. But I suppose I am – I'm on planet parenthood, a bizarre netherworld where everyone talks like idiots and where visiting a family fun pub seems like a good idea. I only hope I'm going to like it here.

· · ·

Back down here on Earth I've just called the new grandparents and my closest friend. Not everyone was entirely tolerant of my witless babbling, which I can't help as I'm so very, very tired. I had trouble remembering the key details of birth weight, exact time of delivery, eye colour and family resemblances. He still doesn't have a name, either. If I was alert enough to care, I'd probably have sympathy for our poor families, sitting and waiting at the other end of a phone line, not knowing the drama that's just unfolded. But I need to eat, drink a large glass of something alcoholic and go to bed with a good book. I should be worried that I'll have trouble sleeping, that I'll just replay the day's events over and over in my head. But to be honest, I wouldn't believe it had happened.

•   •   •

After the thrills and spills of the boy's first day in the world, his second must have seemed like an anticlimax. But for me it was a much more acceptable pace. We've had the whole day together as a family, left in splendid isolation on the side ward. The midwives have popped in for the odd chat and to demonstrate things like bathing and feeding, but otherwise it has just been the three of us.

Lindsay's been a bit tired and pretty overwhelmed all day, but she's got the calm serenity of someone who knows they've done a good job. She's also got the relief of rediscovering her health – as soon as the numbing effect of the anaesthetic wore off, she realised that her mobility problems had seriously diminished. For the first time in weeks, she walked without her crutches. It might not seem like much, but it feels like a minor miracle.

The decision to keep our families at bay was one of the toughest, most rewarding choices we've made. Of course, it depends on them respecting our privacy – they could have just turned up today unannounced, but they've left us to it, though Lindsay's parents must be itching to see their first grandchild. The effect has been that I've taken my first few tentative steps into fatherhood without fear of judgement or criticism. The family will get their chance to meet the new arrival next week, when we're back in familiar surroundings with an established routine.

Getting home is so important to Lindsay, who is now heartily sick of the hospital. We'd initially thought that she might spend a couple of days in a smaller, community hospital run by midwives, but the whole experience has put her right off healthcare. She's begged the powers that be to let her out as soon as possible, and I've promised I'll be on hand to look after her and the boy. They've agreed to an early parole.

Tomorrow I get to drive my wife and son home for the first time. I've spent hours testing the fittings on the child seat, and I'm just about happy with it. I'm nervous and full of pride and anticipation.

So far he's spent most of his time asleep, which is understandable given his sudden and traumatic entry to the world. But he's shown us enough of his fledgling personality to road-test his new name, and it seems to stick.

So it's a big welcome to Oliver Giles. Good luck mate. With a dad like me, you're going to need it.

Epilogue
Merry Xmas everybody

If someone had told me last Christmas that I would be celebrating this year's festivities with my new son, I'd have laughed them all the way to the lunatic asylum. Yet a few short weeks after the traumatic, stunning, unforgettable events of my son's birth it is Christmas again, and life has come around in a full circle as dizzying as any carousel. And despite all the strangeness, somehow it feels as if this is how life has always been.

There have always been stinking nappies and fountains of pee, tiny clothes dripping on the line, monstrous supermarket bills, endless visits from cooing tunnel vision grandparents, sleepless nights and exhausted days. There have always been old-age midwives and new age health visitors, doctors' appointments, frightening baby jabs and endless weighing sessions. There's always been a house crammed to the rafters with plastic toys and fluffy bears. There's always been the dilemma between being a good father and becoming a control freak.

But that's all a different story. This one has come to its happy end.

Contact us

You're welcome to contact White Ladder Press if you have any questions or comments for either us or the author. Please use whichever of the following routes suits you.

Phone: 01803 813343 between 9am and 5.30pm

Email: enquiries@whiteladderpress.com

Fax: 01803 813928

Address: White Ladder Press, Great Ambrook, Near Ipplepen, Devon TQ12 5UL

Website: www.whiteladderpress.com

What can our website do for you?

If you want more information about any of our books, you'll find it at **www.whiteladderpress.com**. In particular you'll find extracts from each of our books, and reviews of those that are already published. We also run special offers on future titles if you order online before publication. And you can request a copy of our free catalogue.

Many of our books also have links pages, useful addresses and so on relevant to the subject of the book. You'll also find out a bit more about us and, if you're a writer yourself, you'll find our submission guidelines for authors. So please check us out and let us know if you have any comments, questions or suggestions.

KIDS&Co

"Ros Jay has had a brilliant idea, and what is more she has executed it brilliantly. **KIDS & CO** is the essential handbook for any manager about to commit the act of parenthood, and a thoroughly entertaining read for everyone else"
JOHN CLEESE

WHEN IT COMES TO RAISING YOUR KIDS, YOU KNOW MORE THAN YOU THINK.

So you spent five or ten years working before you started your family? Maybe more? Well, don't waste those hard-learned skills. Use them on your kids. Treat your children like customers, like employees, like colleagues.

No, really.

Just because you're a parent, your business skills don't have to go out of the window when you walk in throughthe front door. You may sometimes feel that the kids get the better of you every time, but here's one weapon you have that they don't: all those business skills you already have and they know nothing about. Closing the sale, win/win negotiating, motivational skills and all the rest.

Ros Jay is a professsional author who writes on both business and parenting topics, in this case simultaneously. She is the mother of three young children and stepmother to another three grown-up ones.

£6.99

Babies
for Beginners

If it isn't in here, you don't need to know it.

At last, here is the book for every new parent who's never been quite sure what a cradle cap is and whether you need one. **Babies for Beginners** cuts the crap – the unnecessary equipment, the overfussy advice – and gives you the absolute basics of babycare: keep the baby alive, at all costs, and try to stop it getting too hungry.

From bedtime to bathtime, mealtime to playtime, this book highlights the CORE OBJECTIVE of each exercise (for example, get the baby bathed) and the KEY FOCUS (don't drown it). By exploding the myths around each aspect of babycare, the book explains what is necessary and what is a bonus; what equipment is essential and what you can do without.

Babies for Beginners is the perfect book for every first time mother who's confused by all the advice and can't believe it's really necessary to spend that much money. And it's the ultimate guide for every father looking for an excuse to get out of ante-natal classes.

Roni Jay is a professional author whose books include KIDS & Co: winning business tactics for every family. She is the mother of three young children, and stepmother to another three grown up ones.

£6.99

Full Time Father

HOW TO SUCCEED AS A STAY AT HOME DAD

"At last, a hands-on, amusing and above all realistic guide for dads who have given up work to bring up their children. What makes this book so rewarding is that it is written by a father who has been there, seen it and done it."
Nick Cavender, Chairman, HomeDad UK

So your partner earns more than you do?
You've been made redundant? You hate the job?
Being a full time dad can make a lot of sense.

But isn't it a bit weird? Actually no; it's a growing trend. Nearly one in ten fathers in the UK now takes the main responsibility for looking after the kids, often full time.

It's a big decision though. What will your mates think? Will you ever get a decent job again? Won't you miss the cut and thrust of the office? And won't you go stark staring mad without any mental stimulation too sophisticated for a toddler? It's not just you, either. It's the whole family set up. Who wears the trousers? Who controls the family purse? And does it mean you have to clean the house and do the shopping, too?

Full Time Father is written by a stay at home dad and draws on his survey of other 'homedads' as well as on his own experience. It examines all the key issues, passes on masses of valuable tips and advice, and lets the reader know what to expect – both good and bad – should they decide to become a homedad themselves.

£9.99

THE VOICE OF TOBACCO

"An amazing new book on smoking — it has great style and humour, and is brilliantly funny. Read this happy smoker's guide — if only I had been the author."
LESLIE PHILLIPS

What does the Voice of Tobacco say to you?
There's no need to give up; just cutting down will do.
How can it be bad for you when it feels so good?
Just one cigarette can't hurt you, now can it?

It's hard not to listen. Especially when, from the other side of the debate, we smokers have all been lectured by self-righteous prigs who think that (a) we should want to give up and (b) giving up smoking should be easy.

Well we don't and it ain't.

And yet there does come a time when, no matter how much we enjoy smoking, we have to become not smokers.

Richard Craze's guide gives it to you straight: what it's really like to give up smoking. The headaches, the sleeplessness, the irritability. And The Voice. He's been there and his diary reports back from the front line. It may not be pleasant, but it's honest. It may or may not help you to give up smoking, but it will certainly get you looking at smoking in a new way. And it will give you something to do with your hands.

This is the diary of a dedicated and happy smoker who is now not smoking. Here's how he did it. Here's how to do it without the trauma, the withdrawal symptoms, the twitching, the bad temper. Yeah, right. In your dreams.

£6.99

The White Ladder Diaries

> "To start a business from scratch with a great idea but little money is a terrifying but thrilling challenge. White Ladder is a fine example of how sheer guts and drive can win the day."
> **TIM WATERSTONE**

Have you ever dreamed of starting your own business?

Want to know what it's like? I mean, what it's really like?

Ros Jay and her partner, Richard Craze, first had the idea for White Ladder Press in the summer of 2002. This is the story of how they overcame their doubts and anxieties and brought the company to life, for only a few thousand pounds, and set it on its way to being a successful publishing company (this is its third book).

The White Ladder Diaries isn't all theory and recollections. It's a real life, day-by-day diary of all those crucial steps, naïve mistakes and emotional moments between conceiving the idea for a business and launching the first product. It records the thinking behind all the vital decisions, from choosing a logo or building a website, to sorting out a phone system or getting to grips with discounts.

What's more, the diary is littered with tips and advice for anyone else starting up a business. Whether you want to know how to register a domain name or how to write a press release, it's all in here.

If they could do it, so can you. Go on – stop dreaming. Be your own boss.

£9.99

Order form

You can order any of our books via any of the contact routes on page 108, including on our website. Or fill out the order form below and fax it or post it to us.

We'll normally send your copy out by first class post within 24 hours (but please allow five days for delivery). We don't charge postage and packing within the UK. Please add £1 per book for postage outside the UK.

Title (Mr/Mrs/Miss/Ms/Dr/Lord etc)

Name

Address

Postcode

Daytime phone number

Email

No. of copies	Title	Price	Total £
Postage and packing £1 per book (outside the UK only):			
TOTAL:			

Please either send us a cheque made out to White Ladder Press Ltd or fill in the credit card details below.

Type of card ☐ Visa ☐ Mastercard ☐ Switch

Card number

Start date (if on card) _____ Expiry date _____ Issue no (Switch) _____

Name as shown on card

Signature